DESIGN AND MAKE
SOFT
FURNISHINGS

NEW
HOLLAND

This edition first published in 2002 by
New Holland Publishers (UK) Ltd
London • Cape Town • Sydney • Auckland
www.newhollandpublishers.com

Garfield House, 86-88 Edgware Road
London W2 2EA
United Kingdom

80 McKenzie Street
Cape Town 8001
South Africa

Level 1, Unit 4
14 Aquatic Drive
Frenchs Forest, NSW 2086
Australia

218 Lake Road
Northcote, Auckland
New Zealand

10 8 6 4 2 1 3 5 7 9

ISBN 1 85974 150 9

Editor: Tessa Clark
Editorial Coordinator: Kate Latham
Photographer: John Freeman
Designed by: Grahame Dudley Associates and Behram Kapadia
Illustrators: Claire Davies and Lizzie Sanders

Printed and bound in Malaysia by Times Offset (m) Sdn Bhd

CONTENTS

INTRODUCTION

Throws have become one of the most useful accessories in recent years, dressing up a dull dining room chair, or brightening a dreary sofa.

Style is a word which is open to many interpretations and indeed is interpreted differently by each of us. However, when it is present, style is immediately recognisable. Whether our home is a country mansion or an apartment in a large city; whether the architecture is beautiful and inspiring, or whether there is little inherent form and character to the building, we each need to consider and choose a style for our furnishings that reflects our taste and the way we live.

This, of course, is where designing and making soft furnishings comes into its own. Financial savings apart – and these can be considerable – items like curtains and bedcovers, cushions and blinds, loose covers and tablecloths can all be made to your exact requirements and will reflect individual personalities and interests in ways that ones which have been bought in a shop or that are readymade cannot.

Above all, you will have far more options to choose from. But before you make your final choice, take time to decide on the overall effect you wish to create. Do you want a bright and airy living room with sheer curtains that let in the maximum amount of light, and loose covers in fresh cool colours? Or would you prefer a private and enclosed room with heavier, more sumptuous, curtains and tailored covers? Many people like soft colours – creams and/or whites with pinks, pale apricots or light blues – for the furnishings in their bedroom, but others select deeper earthy tones like soft terracotta, olive greens and pinky earth reds. And, of course, you can always make different slip covers or cushion covers for summer and winter.

Fabric for soft furnishings like loose covers and curtains will always have to be bought in bulk, but it is well worth remembering that smaller pieces can be used for decorative accents. Holiday purchases of batik, Indian cottons, brightly coloured South American textiles, and rough woven cottons from Greek islands could be transformed into tablecloths or used to cover a stool. A fabric remnant discovered on a market stall or in an antique shop can be made into a cushion cover, or used for shoe bags or table napkins. Offcuts of furnishing fabric, or the smallest piece of an expensive silk can be used to make truly individual lampshades. A passion for paisley can be indulged in a chair or sofa throw.

Within this book I have tried to cover a cross section of different styles and designs of soft furnishings, to suit as many situations, budgets and tastes as possible. Do not be too daunted if you feel that your house is too small or ordinary: well-dressed furniture and windows are as important in a small apartment as they are in a grand

house, and the general approach to design is the same.

As always, the essence of good design is not how much you can spend on a room or rooms, but what you have done with the

materials available. Above all, start with enthusiasm, take time and great care with the making up of your soft furnishings, and design your own details for that extra finishing touch.

BASIC TECHNIQUES

STITCHES

Start and finish all stitching with a double stitch, never use a knot.

Hemming stitch

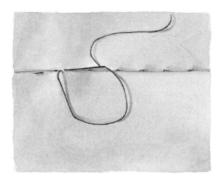

This stitch is used along hems. Each stitch should be approximately 1.5 cm (⅝ in) in length. Slide the needle through the folded hem, pick up two threads of the main fabric, and push the needle directly back into the fold.

Herringbone stitch

Herringbone stitch is used over any raw edge which is then covered by another fabric. It is worked in the opposite direction to all other stitches. Each stitch should be about 3 cm (1¼ in) for hems and 8 cm (3¼ in) for side turnings. Stitch into the hem, from right to left, approximately 1.5 cm (⅝ in) to the right make a stitch into the fabric picking up two threads. Pull through and stitch 1.5 cm (⅝ in) to the right making a stitch into the hem.

Ladder stitch

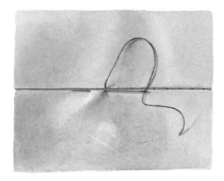

Ladder stitch is used to join two folded edges invisibly together. Slide the needle along the fold 5 mm (¼ in) and straight into the fold opposite. Slide along for 5 mm (¼ in) and back into the first fold, again directly opposite.

Long stitch

Long stitch is the most effective stitch for interlined curtains as it holds the interlining tight to the main fabric on the side turnings.

Make a horizontal stitch approximately 1 cm (⅜ in) across. Bring the thread down diagonally by about 4 cm (1½ in) and repeat.

Slip stitch

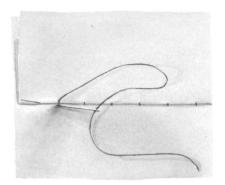

This stitch is used to sew on linings. Always use a colour thread which matches the main fabric. Make each stitch 1.5 cm (⅝ in). Slide the needle through the main fabric and pick up two threads of the lining. Push the needle back into the main fabric exactly opposite and slide through a further 1.5 cm (⅝ in).

Lock stitch

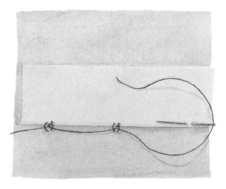

This stitch holds linings, interlinings and fabrics together, preventing them from separating, but still allowing some degree of movement. Always use thread that blends with the main fabric and the lining when stitching lining to interlining. Fold back the lining, secure the thread to the lining and make a small stitch in the main fabric just below. Make a large loop approximately 10 cm (4 in) long (slightly shorter for smaller items) and make a small stitch in the lining inside this loop. Stitch into the main fabric. Allow the stitch to remain slightly loose.

Buttonhole stitch

Work from left to right with the raw edge uppermost. Push the needle from the back to the front, 3 mm (⅛ in) below the edge. Twist the thread around the needle and pull the needle through, carefully tightening the thread so that it knots on the edge.

Blanket stitch

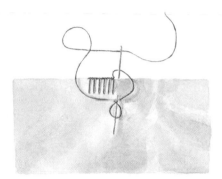

Originally used to neaten the raw edges of woollen blankets, it is now mainly decorative. It is most comfortable worked from the side with the edge towards you. Push the needle from the front to the back, about 6 mm (¼ in) from the edge (also this measurement will vary with large or small items). Hold the thread from the last stitch under the needle and pull up to make a loop on the edge.

PINNING

When pinning two layers of fabric together or piping on to fabric, always use horizontal and vertical pins to keep the fabric in place from both directions. The horizontal pins need to be removed just before the machine foot reaches them and the vertical ones – or cross pins – can remain in place, so the fabrics are held together the whole time.

SEAMS

Flat seam

The most common and straightforward seam for normal use. With right sides together, pin 1.5–2 cm (⅝–¾ in) in from the edge at 10 cm (4 in) intervals. Pin cross pins halfway between each seam pin. These cross pins will remain in place while you are stitching to prevent the fabrics from slipping.

Once machine-stitched, open the seam flat and press it from the back. Turn it over and press from the front. Turn it back over once again and press from the back, under each flap, to remove the pressed ridge line.

French seam

This type of seam is very neat and leaves no raw edges. Use for sheer fabrics or any occasion when the seam might be visible.

Pin the fabrics together with the wrong sides facing. Stitch 5 mm (¼ in) from the raw edges. Trim and flip the fabric over, bringing the right sides together. Pin again, 1 cm (⅜ in) from the stitched edge and stitch along this line to enclose the raw edges. Press from the right side, always pressing the seam in one direction only.

Flat fell seam

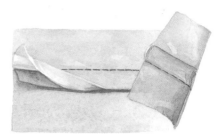

Use for neatening seams of heavier weight fabrics. Pin the fabrics together with the right sides facing and stitch 1.5–3 cm (⅝–1¼ in) from the raw edges. Trim one seam to just under half. Fold the other over to enclose the raw edge. Press down. Stitch close to the fold line.

MITRED CORNERS

This technique creates a flat and neat finish to corners.

When sides and hems are equal

1. Press the side seam over and the hem up, to the measurements given. Position a temporary pin exactly through the point of the corner.

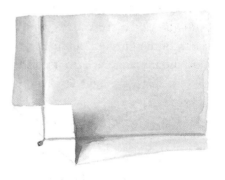

2. Open out the folds and turn in the corner at a 45° angle, with the pin at the centre of the foldline.

3. Fold the hem up and the sides in again along the original fold lines. Keep the pin on the point and make sure the fabric is firmly tucked into the folded lines.

When sides and hems are unequal

Even when this is the case, you can still achieve a neat corner. Follow step 1 as above, but when you reach step 2, the corner will not be folded to a 45° angle.

Instead, the corner will need to be angled away, towards the hem, leaving a longer fold on the side turnings so that the raw edges meet when the mitre is finished.

MAKING TIES

Ties are used throughout soft furnishings. They can be used to close duvets, tie bed cushions, or to secure a headboard cover. For curtains, they can tie a heading to a pole.

Folded ties

Cut a strip of fabric four times the width of your finished tie and 3 cm (1¼ in) longer. Press one short end under by 1 cm (⅜ in) and both sides to the middle. Press in half, and stitch close to the fold line.

Rouleau ties

Cut a strip of fabric four times the width of your finished tie and 3 cm (1¼ in) longer. Fold in half lengthwise, right sides together, enclosing a piece of cord which is longer than the strip of fabric. Stitch along the short side to secure the cord firmly. Stitch along the length, 2 mm (⅛ in) towards the raw edge from the centre.

Trim the fabric across the corner, pull the cord through, at the same time turning the fabric right side out. Cut off the cord. Press the raw edge under and slipstitch with small stitches.

PIPING

If piping is to be used in straight lines then it will be easier to handle straight. If it is to be bent around corners, then it should be cut on the cross. For 4 mm (⅛ in) piping cord cut 4 cm (1½ in) wide strips. All joins should be made on the cross to minimise bulk.

To cut on the straight
Cut lengths as long as possible. Hold two strips, butt the ends together and trim away both corners at 45°. Hold together and flip the top one over. Stitch together where the pieces cross.

To cut on the cross

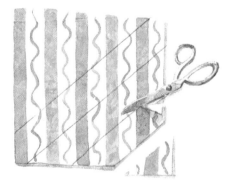

With the fabric flat on the table fold one bottom corner as if making a 30 cm (12 in) square. Cut along the fold line. Mark pencil lines from this cut edge at 4 cm (1½ in) intervals, and cut along these lines. Hold two pieces, butting the ends together as if making a continuous strip. Flip the top one over and hold. Machine stitch together where the two fabrics cross.

Making up and pinning on
Press seams flat and cut away excess corners. Fold in half along the length and insert the piping cord. Machine stitch to encase, approximately 2 mm (⅛ in) from the cord. Keep the fabric folded exactly in half.

Always pin piping so that the raw edges line up exactly with the raw edges of the main fabric.

To bend piping around curves, snip into the stitching line. To pipe around a right angle, stop pinning 1.5 cm (⅝ in) from the corner, snip the piping right to the stitching line, fold the piping to 90° and start pinning 1.5 cm (⅝ in) on the adjacent side.

Joining
To join piping, overlap by approximately 6 cm (2¼ in) and cut away excess. Unpick the casing on one side and cut away the cord so that the two ends butt up. Fold the piping fabric across at a 45° angle and cut along this fold. Fold under 1 cm (⅝ in) and pin securely before stitching.

BINDING

Binding one edge
1. Cut the binding strips to the width required. Join the strips on the cross for the required length.

2. Pin the binding to the fabric, right sides together and stitch slightly less than 1.5 cm (⅝ in) from the raw edges.

3. Neaten the raw edges to slightly less than 1.5 cm (⅝ in). Press from the front, pressing the binding away from the main fabric. Fold the binding to the back, measuring the edge to 1.5 cm (⅝ in), keeping the fabric tucked firmly into the fold and pin at approximately 8 cm (3¼ in) intervals. Turn over to the back and herringbone stitch the edge of the binding to the main fabric, or fold under again.

Binding a corner
If you need to bind a corner, mitre the binding. Stop pinning just short of the corner by the width of the finished binding. Fold the binding back on itself to make a sharp 45° angle and pin across this fold line.

Continue to pin on the adjacent side, the same distance from the edge. Stitch the binding on, stopping right on the pin and secure stitching. Begin stitching again at the same point, on the adjacent side. Press to mitre, and fold the fabric to the back, mitring the corner in the opposite direction to relieve the bulk.

GLUING FABRIC TO CARD

Not all decorative accessories require sewing. Many of the storage boxes and picture frames need to be glued. However, to ensure successful results, always use a PVA glue which is water soluble and which dries clear. The best glue to use will give immediate contact, so do prepare well as mistakes cannot be rectified. Practise first with scraps if you are not confident. Always spread glue on to the card in a thin, even layer. Place the fabric on to the table and press to remove all creases. Place the card on to the fabric, matching up any straight lines or checks along the card sides. Turn over immediately and smooth out any bubbles, checking that fabric has not shifted and the pattern is still matched correctly. However careful you are, there will be the odd stray spots of glue, so keep a slightly damp cloth by your side to wipe away any excess immediately. If you have put too much glue on to the card and it does seep through the fabric, keep wiping the excess away with a damp cloth. Providing you are prompt, the fabric should dry without marking. At each stage, leave the fabric covered card to dry completely. A pile of books or heavy weight on top will prevent the card bowing if the fabric is inclined to shrink. The easiest fabrics to work with are tightly woven, mediumweight, pre-shrunk cottons, but the linens, wools and heavier cottons can be used once you have mastered the basic techniques.

PLACKET WITH TIES

1. Plackets are openings on loose covers. To make, cut one 8 cm (3¼ in) piece of fabric and one 12 cm (4¾ in) wide, each the length of the opening. Stitch the widest one to the back and the narrower one to the side of the chair cover.

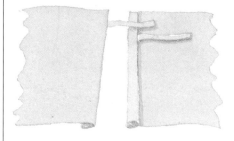

2. Starting with the back, press this wider flap forwards. Measure 3 cm (1¼ in) from the seam line and fold under. Turn over to the back, and fold under another 3 cm (1¼ in) so that the fold lines up with the stitching line on the back and pin. Press the side flap to the back and fold in half to make a hem.

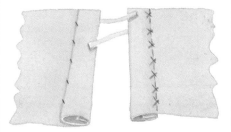

3. Finish the hemline, whether a valance will be attached, a binding or a self hem. Slip stitch along the folded lines with small stitches. Pin the ties in place and insert with the first seam line. Add hooks and bars if you prefer.

INSERTING A ZIP

The first method is very straightforward. The second is used for inserting a zip into a piped seam.

Method 1

1. Pin one side of the zip to the opening, 2 mm (⅛ in) away from the teeth. Machine topstitch this half of the zip in place.
2. Machine the other side of the opening to the zip, forming a flap to encase the teeth.

Method 2

1. Apply piping to the front of the fabric. Join front and back pieces together, allowing a gap for zip.

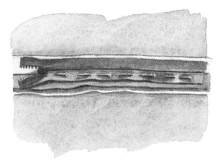

2. Pin one side of the zip against the piping line on the front of the cushion from the wrong side. Machine stitch tightly in place.
3. Open out cushion seam and pin other side of the zip in place, ensuring that the fabric butts up to the piping without gaping. Machine stitch in place, stitching across the ends of the zip to prevent the head of the zip from becoming lost.

CUSHION BORDERS

Cut pieces for the whole cushion. Add 1.5 cm (⅝ in) seam allowance to each cut edge. The centre of the cushion will be cut as a whole panel and the borders stitched along each side, so for an outer border and an inner one you will need to cut 13 pieces for the cushion front.

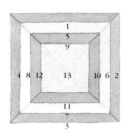

1. Join sides 9/10/11/12 to the centre piece (13) one at a time, stopping and securing stitched 1.5 cm (⅝ in) for each side of each corner.

2. Join 5/6/7/8 to the 9/10/11/12 piece, stitching to the end of each piece. Repeat with sides 1/2/3/4. Press all seams flat.

3. Pin across each corner to mitre, and adjust pins as necessary so that the cushion and each corner sits absolutely flat on to the worktable. Stitch along the pin line and press.

4. Continue to make up following the instructions for plain, piped or bordered cushions.

Cut sizes including seam allowances:

Sides 1/2/3/4	53 x 6 cm (21 x 2¼ in)
Sides 5/6/7/8	47 x 6 cm (18½ x 2¼ in)
Sides 9/10/11/12	41 x 6 cm (16 x 2¼ in)
Centre 13	35 x 35 cm (13¾ x 13¾ in)

CURTAIN WEIGHTS

To ensure that curtains hang and drape well, you should insert weights into curtain hems at each seam and at each corner. Make a lining cover for each weight to prevent it rubbing and possibly discolouring the fabric. Very heavy curtains or sheer curtains should have a length of fabric-covered chain weight threaded into the hem instead. Chain weight is available in different weights to suit all purposes.

DRESSING CURTAINS

Hand-headed curtains need to be dressed as soon as they are hung so that the pleats are trained to fall evenly. You will need to leave the curtains tied back for at least 48 hours and possibly up to 96 hours. The waiting will be well rewarded as your curtains will always hang well.

Begin by drawing the curtains to the stack-back position. Make sure that the heading is in order, the pleats are forwards and the gaps are folded evenly between each pleat. If the curtain hangs under a track or pole, the gaps will fold behind, if in front, the gaps will fold to the front.

Stand at eye level with the headings and take each pleat, smoothing it down through the curtain as far as you can reach to form a fold. Now, standing on the floor or lower down the step ladder and starting at the leading edge, follow these pleats through to waist height. From the leading edge fold each pleat back on to the last. Tie a strip of fabric loosely around the curtain to hold the pleats in place.

Kneel on the floor and follow the folds through into the hem. Finger press firmly. If the curtains are overlong, keep the pleats together and bend the curtain to one side. Tie another strip of fabric around the curtain hems to hold the pleats in place, loosely enough not to mark the fabric, but tight enough so that they do not slip down.

Springy fabrics may need to be readjusted several times, but this will become easier as the pleats are trained.

Instructions for measuring and estimating the amount of fabric required for soft furnishings is given at the back of the book.

Bed furnishings: page 173
Blinds: page 179
Loose covers: page 182
Tablecloths: page 184
Napkins: page 184
Lampshades: page 185
Cushions: page 186
Curtains: page 187

PREPARATION

This is the key to successful sewing. Prepare well, and the work should go smoothly, with few errors. Look at various factors before you begin: where you are going to work, what materials and equipment you plan to use. Here are some guidelines to bear in mind before you begin sewing.

THE WORKTABLE

If possible, you should stake your claim on one room which can be put aside for your own use.

A dining room or guest bedroom can be made into a temporary workroom with little effort. A worktable which is at least 2.5 x 1.2 m (8 x 4 ft) and preferably 3 x 1.5 m (10 x 5 ft) will make the whole job so much easier. You can buy a sheet of board in either of these sizes. Cover your dining table with thick felt so that the board can be rested safely on top.

Alternatively, make some sturdy legs which can be bracketed on to the underside of the board. This quickly made table can then be fitted temporarily over a guest bed. The space below can be used to store all your fabrics, and the top will be wide enough for you to work on a whole width of fabric at a time. Pure luxury compared to hands and knees on the floor! The height of the worktable should be whatever is comfortable for you; I use a table that is 95 cm (38 in) high.

Cover the top with heavy inter-lining and then a layer of lining. Staple these to the underside; pulling the fabrics very taut as you go. You will now have a soft surface which is ideal for pinning and pressing.

CHECKING THE FABRIC

Before you begin to cut the fabric, check it for flaws or incorporate them where they will not be seen. Return a badly flawed fabric.

Measure out each length and mark with pins to make sure that you have the correct amount of fabric. Always double check your measurements before cutting.

Fabric should ideally be cut along the grain and to pattern, but sometimes the printing method allows the pattern to move off grain. If necessary, allow the pattern to run out slightly to either side – but a 2 cm (¾ in) run-off is the most you should tolerate. Make sure that the leading edges of all pairs of curtains match each other exactly.

PATTERN MATCHING

It is well worth spending a little time to make sure that all fabric patterns are matched correctly at the seam on each width.

1. Place one of the lengths of fabric right side up on the worktable with the selvedge facing you. Place the next length over the first, right side down.

Fold over the selvedge to reveal roughly 5 mm (¼ in) of pattern and press lightly.

2. Match the pattern to the piece underneath, and pin through the fold line along the whole length. You may need to ease one of the sides at times – using more pins will help. Go back and place cross pins between each pin. Machine or hand stitch along the fold line, removing the straight pins and stitching over the cross pins.

3. Press the seam from the wrong side and then again from the front. Use a hot iron and press quickly. Turn the fabric over again to the back and press under the seam to remove the pressed ridges. If the background fabric is dark or you are using a woven fabric, snip into the selvedges at 5 cm (2 in) intervals. If it is light, trim the selvedges back to 1.5 cm (⅝ in), removing any printed writing.

PLACING THE PATTERN

On loose chair covers, the pattern should be placed so that it always runs from top to bottom. For this reason the outside and inside arm pieces should never be cut as one. Patterns should run from the top of the inside arm to the seat and from the top of the outside arm towards the floor. Match all patterned or geometric prints at each piping seam.

Plan all fabric pieces so that the pattern follows up through from the floor, across the seat and then up the back.

PLANNING FABRIC CUTS

Loose covers: view the chair as a series of rectangles – inside back, outside back, seat, etc. Measure each piece, allowing 3–4 cm (⅛–1½ in) seam allowance in each direction, plus 10–20 cm (4–8 in) for 'tuck-in', which should be as large as the space allows. Always use a full fabric width at the centre of a cover with panels joined at either side. Seams must follow from the front, across the seat and up through the back.

Curtains and blinds: As you cut each piece, mark the right sides and the direction of a plain fabric. If you have to fold the lengths, make sure it is lengthwise. Join the widths and half widths, using flat seams for lined and interlined curtains and blinds, flat fell seams for heavy, unlined curtains and unlined blinds and French seams for lightweight unlined curtains.

Keep a full width in the centre of blinds and make joins on either side. Trim away any writing on the selvedge, press from the back and then from the front. Then, press again on the back with the toe of the iron between the seam and the front fabric to remove any pressing lines.

Sofa and chair cushions: cushions should always be made to match the position of the pattern on the main body of the sofa or chair cover. If possible, plan enough fabric to make all cushions reversible.

If you have made a paper template of the chair seat or stool, transfer this to calico or scrap fabric and add 2 cm (¾ in) all round for seams. If the cushions are square or rectangular, measure carefully and note the longest and widest measurements. Add 2 cm (¾ in) all around for seam allowances. Measure gussets, frills, piping and note the sizes needed, adding seam allowances.

Plan these pieces (top, bottom, gusset, etc) on the worktable to see how they fit into the fabric width. Plan matching cushions to obtain maximum benefit from the fabric. If this has a dominant pattern, the pieces will need to be planned thoughtfully so that the cushions are cut together to prevent wastage of fabric.

On seat and back cushions, patterns should always read from front to back. The gusset should be placed so that the pattern follows through and matches exactly. Piping may be cut on the cross or on the straight; if there are any curves or curved corners, cut on the cross so that the piping can be bent and still lie flat.

As a general rule, allow 1 m (1 yd) of fabric for each seat. So allow approximately 2 m (2¼ yds) for a two-seat sofa.

Also, remember to allow for pattern repeats when planning your cuts. Small geometric patterns and all-over designs need approximately 10 per cent extra fabric; large prints may need almost double the amount a plain fabric will take to match up correctly. Fabric bindings need to be of similar weight to the main fabric used on the chair, or instead you could use wide ribbon, linen tape or upholstery webbing.

FABRIC WITH BORDERS

Some fabrics have printed or woven borders on one or both sides, so before cutting you need to determine where and how to use them. When the border is on both sides of curtain fabric, decide whether it should appear on the leading and outside edges only, or whether one border should appear at each seam, in which case the extra one should be removed as the widths are joined.

On blinds, borders usually look best around the edges, so cut them all away before joining the widths and then stitch them back on to the blind.

Where there is a border on one side of the fabric only, it should appear on the leading edge of each curtain. Trim the border from the whole length and stitch it back on to each leading edge. If the pattern is directional, pin it back on accordingly.

PREPARING LININGS

Cut out your lining fabric as closely to the grain as possible. Because this is often hard to see, allow about 5 cm (2 in) extra for each cut length. Join all lining widths with flat seams.

For blinds, buy lining the same width as your main fabric or, if it is wider, cut down to match the fabric width before joining. If your curtains have half widths, it is easier to join all whole widths first and then cut the centre width through the middle.

To make up the hems, place one lining on to the worktable, wrong side facing up, with one selvedge exactly along the edge of the table. Turn up approximately 12 cm (4½ in) along the lower edge and press in place. Keep this parallel to the bottom of the table. Trim the hem to 10 cm (4 in) from the fold and then fold it in half to make a 5 cm (2 in) double hem. Pin and machine stitch close to the fold line or slipstitch.

INTERLININGS

It is important that interlining is cut out following the grain. If it is not stitched into the curtain exactly square, after a period of time it will fall down into the hemline. Use the grain line at the headings and hems to help you

Join all widths with flat seams and trim them back to 2 cm (¾ in), snipping into the selvedge at 5 cm (2 in) intervals.

LINING SOFT (UNRODDED) BLINDS

Wherever possible, the lining seams must match the fabric seams. Apart from helping to keep the fabrics straight, all seams show up against the light, so the making methods must be as neat and unobtrusive as possible.

Press all seams flat both front and back to remove any ridges, fold linings lengthwise and rest over a long table or bannister rail to keep everything straight.

LINING RODDED BLINDS

Cut the lining lengths to the length of the finished blind plus 6 cm (2¼ in) for each rod pocket. Join widths to match the main fabric, and trim to exactly the finished blind width. Place the lining on to the worktable with the right side facing down. Press over 3 cm (1¼ in) along each long side.

Starting from the bottom, and using the set square, trim the hemline exactly square with the two sides. Measure from this line up to mark the position of the lower rod pocket, in two rows 5 cm (2 in) apart. Use a set square to keep these lines exactly at right angles to the sides.

Measure from this line to the next, then 6 cm (2¼ in) and repeat to the top. Check that the distance between the top of the blind and the top of the top rod pocket is correct.

Draw a light pencil line at the top and bottom of each rod pocket. Fold together and stitch one each in turn. Press the rod pockets upwards and leave on one side.

PIPING

Piping cord is available commercially in a wide range of thicknesses, graded numerically according to the diameter of the cord, corresponding roughly to the metric measurement of the diameter. Therefore a 5 mm (¼ in) diameter cord is designated

No. 5. No. 00 is the narrowest cord and No. 7 is the widest one that is normally available.

Piping strips should be cut to make a 2 cm (¾ in) seam after the fabric has been folded around the cord. 5 cm (2 in) strips will fit No. 4 cord, which is the most generally used size.

Tiny pipings are used for decorative work and in places where piping is desirable but a thick edge of colour is not. Chunky piping cords are used where a definite statement is needed and they can be very effective if you are piping in the same fabric as the cushion or seat cover: the size of the cord, rather than a contrast in colour, makes the detail.

CUTTING CARD OR MAT

If you have self healing board all well and good, if not, it is probably not worth buying one, so use a piece of glass or board instead. Your knife will blunt a little more quickly, but blades cost considerably less than cutting boards. Either a Stanley knife or a small craft knife is suitable for cutting, but remember that the blade must be very sharp.

A set square and a steel ruler are essential to keep the lines and corners straight. Mark your cutting lines in pencil and cut from back to front, scoring once along the pencilled line first, and then once more to cut through.

A small sanding block covered with fine sandpaper can be made up and used to smooth any rough or uneven edges.

LIVING ROOMS

Good use was made of the printed fabric border. Instead of a skirt, flaps stitched to the border fabric between each leg have been tucked underneath and tied at each corner.

The period of your home and your way of life will have the most influence on how you style your living room, but fashion and furnishing trends should be considered so that your ideas are not quickly out-dated. This applies particularly to making your own loose covers - a considerable investment in time and money - so watch out particularly for trends in mixing colours and fabrics. Choose a 'second' fabric with a tone just deeper than the main one for a formal cover, a soft tone with a floral pattern or self-piping for an informal one, and a check on the cross or stripe for impact. Cotton, whether fine lawn or heavy velvet, makes up and wears with impunity. Linen union is a blend of cotton and linen fibres and is often hailed as the perfect loose cover fabric, but in time the stronger threads cut into the weaker. Printed pure linens are the most forgiving and good tempered fabrics, perfect for both professionals and beginners.

Loose covers - confusingly they may fit so tightly that they cannot be distinguished from upholstered ones, or be loose enough to slip on or off or be draped - are the major consideration in a living room and this chapter concentrates on providing a selection of covers for all tastes: tailored and loose fitting, for armchairs, stools and even wooden chairs. But they are not the only soft furnishing elements in the room and cloths to cover display tables, and ideas for a variety of lampshades - focal points in any design scheme - are also included.

TAILORED COVERS

Excellent for formal-style sofas, chairs and stools and traditional rooms, tailored covers look upholstered but may be removed for laundering. Ideally they should fit so tightly that not a wrinkle can be seen, so care must be taken when working on shapes like arms and wings. Tailored covers are normally easier to make if they are fitted tightly but made up with some easement -- so that a wobbly seam or uneven cut is disguised. Although not essential, skirts or valances like the one above are useful both to disguise poor legs and to alter the impact of a chair or sofa.

Cutting out the Cover

Refer to pages 13–14 and 182–83 before you begin in earnest and practise with a toile if you are nervous. Loose covers must always be fitted with the fabric pinned in place right side out, i.e. as it will look when finished. This is because not only are there never two chairs exactly the same, neither are the left and right sides of any one chair exactly the same!

1. Fold the inside back piece in half lengthwise, with the right sides of the fabric together. Finger press lightly. Line the fold line against the centre line of the chair and pin at top and bottom. Open out the piece and pin at 10–20 cm (4–8 in) intervals to anchor to the side and top of the chair. Pins should be at right angles to the chair with the points inwards. Repeat with the outside back, anchoring it to the sides and bottom of the chair frame as well.

2. Holding the fabric firmly between finger and thumb, pin the pieces together along the back edge of the chair. Remember that the pin line will be the seam/piping line. Pins should be in a straight line, nose to tail, right against the furniture to give an accurate line for stitching later. Start and finish 4–6 cm (1½–2¼ in) above the arm on both sides. Pin from the back of the chair, and ease the front piece around shaped backs, making darts or small tucks at the corners.

3. Position the inside and outside arm pieces of one arm on to the chair, checking the pattern is in the right place, and keeping the grain straight, vertically and horizontally. The pattern and grain of the outside arm should be level with the floor not the top of the arm.

Pin these pieces together along the arm, making some allowance for any arm curvature. The seam may be at the top of the arm, on the outside of the arm or under the scroll, depending on the actual arm style of the chair. Repeat with the other arm.

4. Pin the arm fronts to the chair, checking that the grain is straight. Fix the position with two crossed pins. Anchor all around, with pins at right angles to the chair, points inwards.

5. Pin the inside and outside arm pieces to the arm front, easing curves and fullness. Some arms will have no fullness to disperse, other arms will need one or two darts at this point, but mostly the excess fabric will be eased in with small gathers or pleats, spread evenly around the curved section.

6. Pin the outside arm pieces to the chair back piece. Joining the back arm to the inner back is the trickiest part so should be practised with spare calico if you are a beginner. If you over-cut the seam, the cover will be too tight and if you under-cut, too loose. Fold the inside back piece up so that the fold line marks the seam from the top of the arm to the back. Fold the arm piece to make the opposite side of the seam.

7. Cut away the excess fabric to 3–4 cm (1¼–1½ in) seam allowance as far as the start of the curve of the arm and the seat back (do not cut this too tightly yet in case some adjustment is needed). Make marking tacks with contrast thread three or four times along the folds at exactly opposite points so that the pieces can be matched accurately for seaming.

8. Pencil a line around the arm curve and down into the seat. Trim 3 cm (1¼ in) away from this pencil line where there is no tuck-in space and approximately 10 cm (4 in) where there is. Do the same with the inner arm. Either pin the fabrics together along the pencilled line or fold each back on themselves. The actual shape of the arm and the extent of the curve will make one of these methods easier than the other. Snip right into the seam allowances where necessary for the fabric to lie flat. Gradually cut the seam allowance back to 2 cm (¾ in).

9. Trim the whole cover, leaving a 2 cm (¾ in) seam allowance all around. Cut V-shaped balance marks so that the pieces can be easily matched for stitching.

10. Stitch individual tailor tacks in contrasting thread to each piece at the actual meeting point of the arm seam with the arm front, and at any other area where they might be useful for matching the pieces before stitching. Repeat with the other arm.

11. Place the seat piece on to the chair seat, again matching the centre fold to the pinned line, and anchor all around.

12. Fold the two sides over along the length of the arms, so that the fold lines join the arm fronts at the edge of the front of the chair. Pin the front gusset to the front of the chair, checking that it is centred and level with the floor. Pin the top of this piece to the seat piece along the front edge. Where these two pieces meet the arm front, push a pin through all three pieces so that there is a definite point at which all pieces will meet when stitched. Mark each piece individually with a secure tack in contrast thread at this point.

13. Pin the front gusset to the arm fronts, from the marked join to the bottom of both pieces. Measure and mark the folded back sides of the seat piece so that the tuck-in is equal from front to back along the length of the arm. Cut carefully along this line.

14. Pin the inside arm pieces to the seat piece for approximately 20 cm (8 in) from the front towards the back, cutting back and shaping the join to correspond with the available tuck-in allowance.

15. Using a wooden ruler, measure up from the floor all around to the skirt position. Mark with pins. Allow for the seam allowance and cut the excess fabric away. At this point, if the chair needs to have a back opening, fold back the outside arm piece and the back piece to allow the necessary easement. Pin the fabric back on itself to keep the fold. Mark the top of the opening with a tack on each piece.

16. Tidy up and cut all seam allowances so that they are equal. (If you have accidentally under-cut at any point, mark the place, so that you can adjust the seam allowance to compensate when pinning the pieces, together.) Make sure that you have snipped enough balance marks. Use single, double and triple cuts to make matching easier. Remove the anchor pins and lift the cover off.

Wings

The wing of an armchair or sofa, however small, usually needs to be cut quite separately from the rest of the cover.

1. Cut out pieces for the backs and arms as before. Pin the inner and outer chair backs together along the top of the chair. Pin each piece securely to the upholstery beneath. Cut and fit the arms.

2. For each wing, cut two squares, one for the inner and one for the outer side. Measure carefully – the distance between the back and front of the inner wing can be deceptive.

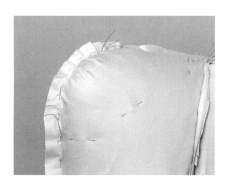

3. Pin each piece securely to the upholstery beneath, taking care to keep the grain straight. Use enough pins so that the centre line remains straight when pulled from both sides. Pin the pieces together around the front shaped edge, easing and snipping as necessary to make a good tight fit. Pin the length of the outside wing to the outside back.

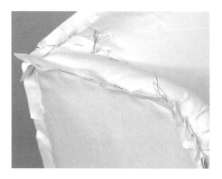

4. Pin the inner wing and chair front pieces together at the top, making cuts and folding seam allowances as needed for the fabric to lie flat. Some wing chairs need the seam to angle back to the corner, but most will run straight from the point of tuck-in to 2–3 cm (¾–1¼ in) from the outside corner.

5. Push your hands into the tuck-in gap (the space between the wing and the inside back) to see how deep it is and where to start and stop the tuck-in.

Originally, this wing chair was upholstered rather severely. A new loose cover creates a more relaxed look.

MAKING UP

If you want the cover to be loose, you will need to stitch so that the seam allowance is less than that allowed, i.e. a stitched seam allowance of 1.5 cm (⅝ in) of the 2 cm (¾ in) allowed in cutting will give 5 mm (¼ in) easement on each side of the seam. It is usual to pin the piping so that the front of the cord is on the seam allowance to give some easement.

The instructions here are for a 'tight' cover like the one on page 17 with the stitching of the piping pinned along the seam allowance.

Make your own adjustments as you prefer, keeping them consistent throughout the making up. Always work with small areas at a time so that there is a limited amount of the unstitched cover unpinned at any one time.

1. Take the pins from one of the seams joining the inside arm to the back. These seams are probably the most vulnerable to movement and fraying so should be stitched and secured first. Turn inside out. Starting at the back, carefully match the tacks, and the ends of the easement cuts. Pin the seam down to the seat. Stitch, reinforcing the curve line by stitching two rows very close together. Do not be afraid to stitch right next to the cuts. If you give these too much berth the cover will not fit back as well as it came off. Neaten the seam. Repeat with the other side.

2. Next unpin one of the arm seams. If piping is to be used on the seam, pin the piping to the right side of the outside arm piece. Stitch in place. Pin the inside arm to the piping line, right sides together, so that the seam allowances and notches match. Stitch. Pin along the piping line and at right angles to it. The pins along the piping must be removed as the machine approaches, but the others can remain in place, preventing the two layers of fabric 'walking'. Stitch in place as close to the piping as possible. Check from the front that the previous stitching line is not visible.

If you have used piping, pull the cord from inside the case at each end for 2 cm (¾ in). Cut the cord away so that the casing lies flat beyond the point at which the back and arm front seam will cross. Neaten the seam. Repeat with the other arm.

3. Unpin the front gusset. Turn inside out, pin the piping along the gusset piece and stitch. At the join with the arm front, pull the cord from the piping case 2 cm (¾ in). Cut away the cord so that the case is flat beyond the tack mark. Pin the right side of the seat piece to the piping line, matching seam allowance and notches. Stitch the length of the piping, between the tack marks. Secure stitches firmly at each end. Neaten this seam.

4. Unpin the sides of the seat from front to back. Turn inside out and pin together again, matching notches and seam allowance. Stitch from the front tack mark to the seam at the back.

5. Unpin one of the front arms. Turn inside out. Pin piping all around the arm, to the right side of the fabric, snipping piping at 1 cm (⅜ in) intervals to ease around any curve. Make sure that you have pinned the piping to give a good shape, and stitch. Pin the inside arm, outside arm and the front gusset to the arm front, matching seam allowances and balance marks. Pin the arm seam so that it is pressed downwards.

6. Ease any fullness carefully. Stitch from the bottom of the front gusset up to the join with the seat. Finish with the needle in the tack mark. Secure with backward and forward stitches to this point. Lift the cover away from the machine. Fold over the seam and start again, with the needle in the tack mark from the other side of the seam.

7. Stitch all around. Look at the stitching line from the front. You might find it quite hard to get close to the piping the first time, because of the joint difficulties of the curve and the fullness. Stitching a small section at a time, slowly stitch as close to the piping as you can, so that the previous stitching line is not visible from the front. Neaten the seam. Repeat with other arm. Ease one fabric on to the other. Shown above is the scroll arm.

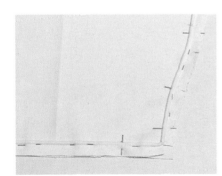

8. Repeat the same stitching process on the centre back, remembering to stitch just a small amount at a time.

9. Unpin the back piece. Pin the piping to the right side of the fabric from just above each arm. Snip to ease where necessary and stitch in place.

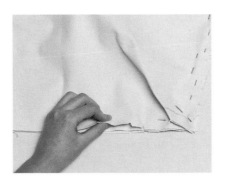

10. Pin the front to the back piece along the piping line. Use plenty of pins, pinned at right angles to the piping to ease any fullness. At the top corners make sure that the hand-stitched or darted corners lie flat and that the finishing off stitches are inside the seam allowance. Stitch as close to the piping as possible.

11. Sleeve the cover back on to the chair. Check that the seam lines are good and re-stitch any that aren't satisfactory.

12. Check that the hemline is still straight and an even distance from the floor. Make the back opening placket if needed (see page 10). Make up a valance or skirt and stitch to the hemline. Stitch the end of the placket to enclose the raw edges at the end of the valance. Fix hooks and bars or ties (see page 10).

13. Press all seams from the front over a damp cloth. Press out the cover and ease back on to the chair. Make sure that the seams all lie in the same direction. Ease the cover around curves and corners. Finger press piping lines to straighten. You will need to spend time easing and fitting the cover into place to obtain the best fit.

Loose covers transform a dining room chair. This bright check can be removed and cleaned easily.

DESIGN AND MAKE SOFT FURNISHINGS

Arm Shapes

It is rare to find two arms that are exactly the same size on an old armchair or sofa, and it is also often the case on a new one. Small differences on new arms are not easy to spot, but still each arm will need to be cut out separately.

The rounded club arm extending to a slight 'wing' (left) shows one of the many and varied arm and side combinations which you might find. The importance of good straight piping lines, evenly spaced, is apparent.

Old arms will misshapen with use over the years and almost always one arm has been flattened more than the other. Small upholstery repairs might be needed – a little re-padding and tightening of the top cover, for example – but much can be disguised by a well-thought-out and fitted loose cover.

Your priority must be to keep the piping lines that run the length of the arm very straight and positioned in the best place. It is difficult to give much direction on this because there are so many arm shapes. On a scroll arm, the seam could be almost at the top or right on the side (see below); on a club arm the seam should give a clear edge, and on a laid back arm the seam could be along the most prominent edge or tucked down into the outside roll. Pin the two arm pieces together in several positions or alternatively draw pencil lines along the arm to help you visualise.

THE STRAIGHT ARM

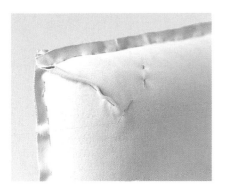

The traditional straight arm or Victorian 'laid back' arm can both be treated in this way. A pinned and stitched dart is the preferred finish for a sharp corner, but if the arm is more rounded than this one, then controlled pleats can be a most attractive way to ease the fullness of the inside arm piece.

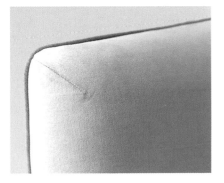

THE CLUB ARM

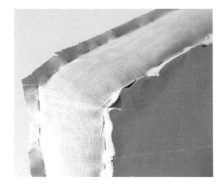

The club arm needs to have its form identified with very straight piping lines. The distance between the piping lines on the front arm and along the top arm must be measured accurately so that the gusset takes priority in the fitting. Any lumps and bumps must be taken up in the side panels.

THE SCROLL ARM

Scroll arms can be fat or thin, short or tall, squidgy or firm. Use your eye to make a good front shape and allow the front piece to take priority in the fitting. To make a misshapen arm beautiful, stitch piping on to the front arm piece first and then pin the sides to the defined line.

Fitted Stool Covers

Stools are useful small accessories in any living room, providing valuable additional seating.

Fitted stool covers benefit from the inclusion of a gusset of some depth to hold the cover firmly over the top 'cushion'. A skirt can then be attached to reach the floor or, if the legs are good, just long enough to cover the upholstery.

If the stool design suggests just a top and skirt, stitch tapes into each corner long enough to tie underneath, so preventing the cover sliding around.

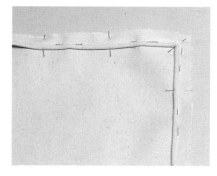

1. Measure, plan and cut the top, gusset and skirt pieces following the principles on pages 182-183. Make up the skirt (opposite), marking each corner clearly. Make up enough piping to fit twice around the stool. Place the top piece on to the worktable and pin the piping around. Keep the corners square and join neatly following the instructions given on the opposite page.

Always plan and design any cover to suit your fabric. These boxed pleats have been placed to do full justice to both small and large teddies.

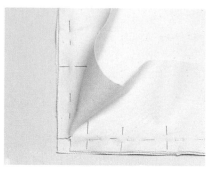

2. Stitch in place. Pin the gusset to the piping line, snipping into the corners sharply, keeping the fabric flat to either side. Join the gusset seam. Stitch along the piping stitching line. Check from the right side to make sure that the first stitching line does not show and if it does, stitch around again closer to the piping.

3. Stitch the remaining piping to the bottom of the gusset. Pin the valance around and tack securely.

4. Fit the cover on to the stool to make sure the length is correct. Stitch close to the piping and again if any stitches still show from the front of the cover.

Skirts and Valances

Decide the depth you wish the valance to be. Add seam allowances of 2 cm (¾ in) for the top and 6 cm (2¼ in) for the hem. Measure the sides, front and back of the chair separately. Plan your valance to fit the four sides. Corner-pleated valances are arguably the most used, the simplest to make and ideal for formal situations.

Corner-pleated valance

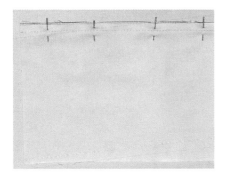

1. Add 40 cm (15¾ in) for the pleats at each corner. Allow 3.5 cm (1⅜ in) to one back piece for the underlap if there is a back opening. Plan to cut each section so that there are no visible seams. Sofa valances will need to have seams either side of the central width on the front and back sections, following those on the seat and outer back seams. It should be possible to hide all other seams inside the pleats at each corner.

Cut the lining to match. Seam the short sides and press flat. Stitch the lining and top fabric together along the length, 1.5 cm (⅝ in) from the lower edge.

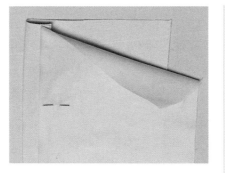

2. Press the seam towards the lining so that fabric bulk is kept to a minimum. Press the main fabric over to the lining side by 3 cm (1¼ in). Pin together and press lightly from the front.

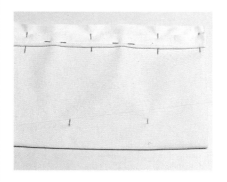

3. Handstitch the short ends. On the right side, measure and mark out each side and each pleat. Pin pleats in position and tack to hold. Pin piping along the top edge. Stitch. Pull the cord away at each end and fold the raw ends inwards.

4. Stitch the valance to the chair cover. If there is a back opening on the cover, first neaten the raw ends at the top of the underlap by carefully slip stitching the bottom of the placket over.

Frilled valance

1. Add measurements of the four chair sides together and multiply by fullness required – usually two to two-and-a-half times. Add 5 cm (2 in) for any underlap at the back. Divide figure by the fabric width, and cut widths required for this length. Cut lining the same depth and enough widths for same length.

2. Join seams and press flat. Pin main fabric and lining together along one long side. Stitch 1.5 cm (⅝ in) from edge. Press hem 4 cm (1½ in) to back. Pin together along top edge. Stitch a gathering thread 1.5 cm (⅝ in) down. Divide length of valance into eight and mark each section with a marking tack. Divide cover hem into eight sections and mark. Match marking tacks and ease gathers evenly. Stitch close to piping – two rows are probably needed to come close enough to cover first stitching line.

Binding the hem

1. Cut fabric strips four times the finished binding width, e.g. 6 cm (2½ in) wide for a 1.5 cm (⅝ in) bound edge. Cut valance and lining fabrics plus 1.5 cm (⅝ in) for a top seam allowance but not at bottom. Stitch lining to one long side and valance fabric to the other, 1.35 cm (just over ½ in) from raw edges. Press both seams towards binding, and from front to remove puckers.

2. Fold binding in half and press. Pin top of both fabrics together.

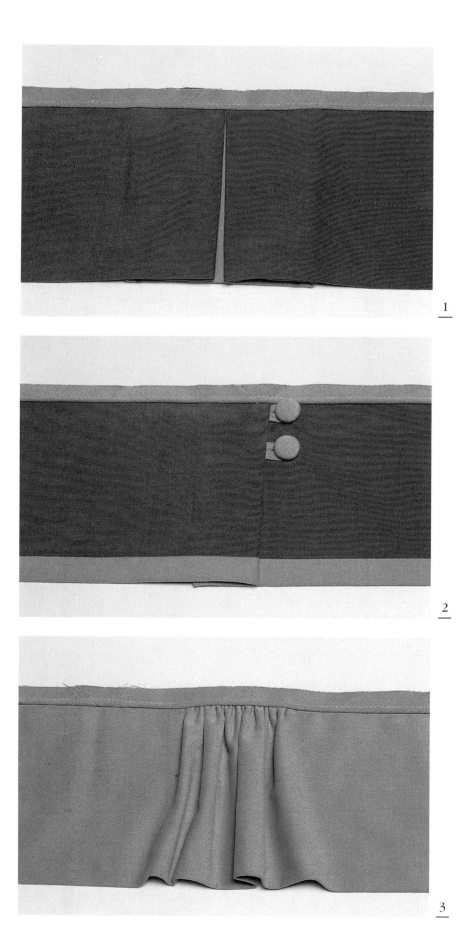

Skirt Selection

When the sofa or chair has been piped with an alternative fabric, whether a contrasting colour, say blue and white, or a toning contrast such as deep pink on soft pink, or a complementary fabric such as a small check on a floral print, the same theme will continue to the skirt. Perhaps just one row of piping at the top will be all that is needed, but binding the hem serves to 'weight' the skirt. Buttons with loops or buttonholes, poppers, ties, frogging and many other dressmaking finishes can be used to decorate the corners of the skirts, as long as the method allows each skirt section to remain sharp at each corner.

Binding the hem might have a more practical use when, for example, the main fabric has a rose print on a light ground and the piping fabric is a deeper tone, as the deeper edge disguises dirt picked up from the floor.

1. Contrast piping and inset pleats smarten up a simple corner-pleated valance/skirt.
2. Each valance/skirt section is made up separately with the sides cut 10 cm (4 in) longer at the front and back so that these sections can overlap. Make rouleau loops and stitch at the end of the valance between the top fabric and the lining. The contrast edgings and details are optional and, depending on the room style, can be sharply contrasting or gently toning.
3. Cut the valance in one long

length, adding approximately 16 cm (6¼ in) to gather around each corner – this is a softer alternative to a pleat.

4. A frilled valance gives a soft and homely finish to a country-style or casual sofa. Contrast binding and piping are not necessary but can make all the difference. Choose mid-toned, plain colours to go with patterned fabrics, a small print or stripe with a larger all-over print, or closely toned plain colours.

5. Knife-pleated skirts fill the gap between the informal, feminine frilled valance and the formal, masculine straight skirt. Allow three times the fullness and make each pleat so that it starts right where the last finished. They are approximately 4 cm (1½ in) wide. Plan them to fit exactly between two chair corners. This means that the pleat sizes might vary slightly on each side but this should not be at all noticeable.

6. Box pleats are made in the same manner as knife pleats. Allow three times fullness, pleat each one against the next and divide equally between the sides so that a chair corner always fits at the centre of a pleat.

Box pleats, knife pleats, inverted pleats and tapered pleats are traditional skirt finishes for both formal and informal situations. Formal rooms and severe furniture will require fewer, very tailored pleats; cottage style furniture needs pleating to be informal, so smaller pleats which kick out playfully rather than standing side by side in strict rows, are probably preferable.

4

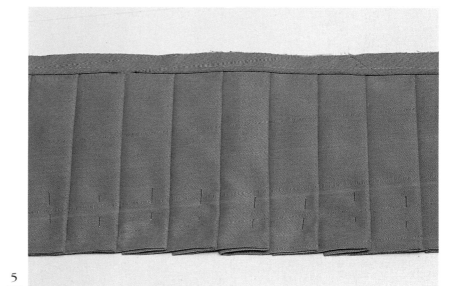

5

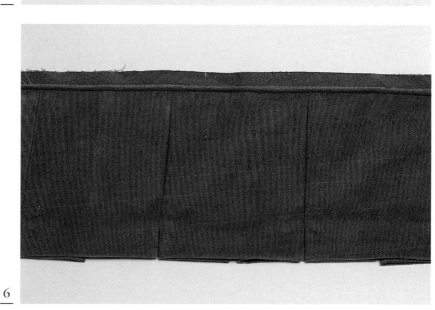

6

Armchair Details

1. Gingham check from hotel suppliers is certainly inexpensive and hard wearing, being manufactured specifically for intensive use and laundering.

Shaped to fit along the top roll and around the arms, the bottom and back were left loose for informality and ease of removal. This chair in my kitchen suffers daily abuse from children and pets, but after constant washing and pressing still looks good.

Flat piping and the back ties are interesting details.

2. Although cut to fit the chair, a nursery cover needs to be casual and simple to slip on and off for cleaning. For ease, the arms were made slightly loose and the skirt frilled from the seat. Nursery fabrics must be washable – I always think it is safer to pre-wash. Most fabrics will shrink a little in both directions, so don't just allowing extra on the length. Remember also only to use pre-shrunk piping cords and to launder linings before cutting.

3. Another chair in the same nursery asked for a different treatment. Inset gussets at each corner have piped sides which spring out to give body and shape to the skirt hem. The cover was pinned to fit the chair as a tailored cover, but each seam was eased 1 cm (⅜ in) before trimming.

4. Ticking is hard-wearing and available in interesting colours and varied stripes. Antique tickings from northern France, hand-woven cloths from Mediterranean islands and other ethnic weaves are often tough enough to make good covers. Some tightly woven fabrics can be hard to pin and stitch. Also check out the creasing factor – crush a square in your hands and see how quickly creases fall out. Always pre-launder an unknown fabric.

5. This idea was taken from an old, favourite jacket – two fabrics with the same weight and fibre content cover an antique French chair whose velvet upholstery I did not wish to remove. Fabric-covered buttons and hand-stitched buttonholes reflect further details.

6. Playing with contrasting fabrics and turning stripes are part of the fun of making loose covers. Centre seams are essential in this chair to take up the back curve.

1

2

3

4

5

6

LIVING ROOMS: TAILORED COVERS

LOOSE FITTING COVERS

These are useful for chairs with wooden frames. Draped covers (overleaf) make pleasant seasonal alternatives to tailored ones.

Loose fitting covers are made, and fabric pieces are planned, as for upholstered chairs. Each piece must be pinned to the chair for the fitting and then together along the seam line.

Use fabric lengths or woven tapes to bind the frame. On a free piece of wood, tapes can be tied around and knotted or pinned in place (see page 60). They must be tightly fixed or they may swivel when you pull on the fabric.

You can stick small pieces of woven tape to a tatty frame, but if the upholstery meets it you will have to pin tapes to the upholstery on either side, stretched taut over the wood. You might be able to use tacks or drawing pins to hold the tape to the underside of the chair. If all else fails, you will have to bandage the chair from top to bottom and side to side.

For seat covers, make a seat template (see page 183) and cut two pieces of linen with a 1.5 cm (⅝ in) seam allowance all around. Make up two skirts, one to fit between the back legs and one for the rest of the seat.

Prepare piping (see page 9) and stitch to one of the seat pieces, 1.5 cm (⅝ in) from the raw edges. Gather the skirts to fit and stitch to the seat along the piping stitching line. Pin rouleau ties to either side of the back legs, and stitch securely with several rows of a zigzag or back stitch. Place the other seat piece over, right sides together, enclosing all seams. Stitch together, leaving a small opening at the back. Neaten seams, cut away corners and snip into curves. Turn out, press and slip stitch the opening.

Right: Organza is draped over the chair and knotted at the back to add a frothiness which can be fun for some occasions.

Below: Seat covers for a set of antique French dining chairs protect the upholstery beneath. Crisp white linen launders easily, returning fresh time and again. An organdie border is stitched to the line with a decorative stitch in perlé thread.

Draped Covers

1. Take measurements and plan cuts as pages 182–83. For this cover, the inner and outer back pieces are cut as one, with 50 cm (20 in) extra allowed at each side. The inner and outer arm pieces are also cut as one, with 40 cm (16 in) extra allowed at the front arm and 20 cm (8 in) at the back. The seat piece is extended at the front and sides to fall to the floor.

2. Make up Turkish or wrap-around cushion covers (see overleaf). Make up four bows each about 20 × 8 cm (8 × 3 in).

3. Join seams as necessary and pin the back and seat pieces to the sofa. Pin together along the back tuck-in. Cut away at the arm front so that the side falls straight. Pin the hem in place along the floor. Trim the fabric along the seat/arm join so that 12 cm (4¾ in) only remains – this for the side tuck-in.

4. Pin the arm piece in place along the top of the sofa arm, and smooth down the inner arm to the seat tuck-in. Pin together along the tuck-in.

5. At the back of the outside arm, pin the 'flap' to the back of the sofa. Pin the back and arm pieces together to shape around the arm. This area needs to be cut well enough so that the arm and back fabrics lie comfortably, but the particular fitting needed for a tight cover is not necessary.

6. Stitch the tuck-ins and arm/back seam together. Neaten seams. Fit the cover back on to the sofa. Shape the excess fabric at the front arm so that the hemline drapes into a gentle curve to the floor. Gather the back pieces together and cut the hemline to drape softly. Remove the cover again and hem these and all other raw edges. Press thoroughly and fit the cover back on to the sofa.

7. Gather the fullness of each drape and stitch with double thread to hold. The flap which is at the back of each side should be pinned to the sofa back with upholstery pins, allowing the folds to hang over the back opening. Stitch rouleau bows over the gathering stitching.

Silk - spun and woven in the manner of linen - is convincing with its crunchy texture and matt finish, and is given away only by the extravagantly soft drapes. Fresh green revives the deep tan under-cover for spring and summer use.

SEAT COVERS

TURKISH CUSHIONS

Turkish cushion covers fit over boxed pads but lend an informal air. The fronts and backs are cut to fit over the pad and meet along the centre line of the gusset. The easiest way to make sure the corners are perfect is to fit the cover over the cushion pad. Once the four sides are pinned, take up the corner excess with a single pleat, an inverted pleat or a series of small gathers. Self-pipe, or hand stitch cord over the seam. Finish with a knot at each corner.

WRAP-AROUND COVERS

Informal and easy-to-make cushion covers, suitable for the complete amateur and those frightened of piping, wrap-around covers depend only on side gussets and a simple closure.

Cut one length of fabric from the centre back gusset along the cushion length, under and around to meet at the centre back. Allow 2 cm (¾ in) at each end for closure allowance. Cut the fabric to the cushion width plus 2 cm (¾ in) seam allowance on each side. Pin over the pad and adjust the back closure seam for a good fit. Remember that the pad is always approximately 10 per cent larger than the finished cover, so fit the cushion into the chair seat to check the fit.

Cut a gusset for each side, the depth and length of the cushion side plus seam allowances. Pin the gussets along each side, keeping the back ends square but easing the fronts to make curved ends. Adjust until a good fit is obtained, trim seam allowances to 2 cm (¾ in), and mark at regular points with coloured tacks. These will help you to realign the pieces once the pins have been removed.

Insert a zip or make a placket for hooks and bars or ties along the closure seam. Open up and pin the side gussets in place, making sure the easement at each gusset front is neat, and any marking tacks are matched. Stitch together, neaten seams and then turn right side out.

If you would like to pipe the side gussets, do so before pinning them back to the main cover.

Wrap-around cushion covers with side gussets are informal and suit squashy country chairs and sofas. Useful also for window seats and Lloyd Loom style chair seats, they are often buttoned through.

DISPLAY TABLECLOTHS

Display tables are important as functional pieces of furniture but can also be used to harmonise colour and weight within a room. The cloth, therefore, must balance the room colourings and style, be an item in its own right and still perform the duty of leading the eye to the display on top. The colour and texture of fabrics need to be carefully considered.

MAKING UP

For a circular cloth

Cut fabric pieces allowing 1.5 cm (⅝ in) for all seams and 3 cm (1¼ in) for the hem. Join widths as necessary – always keeping a full width for the centre panel with seams at either side.

1. Cut and join any lining or interlining. Fold the seamed fabric into four, making sure layers are absolutely flat. From the centre, measure and mark the tablecloth radius, including the hem allowance. Pencil a continuous line between the marks. Cut through all four layers, along this line.

2. Press the hem allowance to the wrong side, pinning to ease the fullness. Herringbone stitch all around, using stitches approximately 1.5 cm (⅝ in) in length.

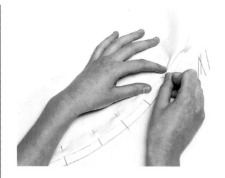

3. Place the lining over, matching up the seams. Lock stitch the two fabrics together along the seams. With the end of your scissors, score the lining, following around the circumference of the cloth. Trim to this line. Fold under 1.5 cm (⅝ in) and slip stitch the lining in place.

Interlining

Interlining adds body and weight to a cloth, improving the drape considerably. A fine fabric can be made to feel heavy and a textured fabric can be given extra depth. Choose interlining which is similar in content to the main fabric. Another advantage with adding interlining is that there are no stitches visible from the front.

Cut and join widths as for the main fabric. Place on to the top fabric, wrong sides facing and lock stitch together along the seams. Trim the interlining hem so that it finishes 3 cm (1¼ in) inside the main fabric and herringbone the raw edge in place. Fold the main fabric hem over and herringbone to the interlining. Line as before in step 3.

Hems

Tablecloths hang and drape better if the hem has some weight to it. Cord, braid or fringing can provide the necessary substance. Applying a bought trimming is less time-consuming than making bound edges or frills, but tends to be more expensive.

Adding cord

Slip stitch cord to the very edge of the hem – in fact take the stitches right into the fold line. Pick up a couple of threads from the cord, keeping the stitches even. Stitches should be tight enough so that the cord does not gape, but loose enough that the fabric does not pucker.

Applying braid

Stitch braid on from both sides. Use a small running stitch in the same direction as the woven braid, matching the thread exactly.

To make a bound hem

Cut the cloth fabric without adding the hem allowance. Cut and join a bias strip from the binding fabric 6 cm (2¼ in) wide and as long as the circumference of the cloth.

1. Pin the binding to the hem, right sides together and stitch 12 mm (½ in) from the raw edges. Use the machine foot to give you an accurate guide.

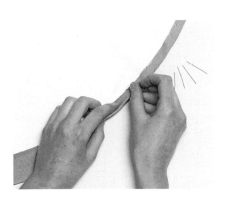

2. Press the edging fabric away from the cloth and fold under, making sure that an even 1.5 cm (⅝ in) is showing.

3. If the cloth is to be lined, herringbone stitch all around.

If interlined, add the interlining as before (see page 38) and stitch to the seam rather than the fold in the binding.

4. Place the lining over, matching seams, and lock stitch together along the seam lines. Score the lining all around the hemline with the point of your scissors. Trim carefully along this line. Fold 1.5 cm (⅝ in) under and slip stitch to the binding. The lining fold should run along the binding seam line.

If unlined, fold the binding in twice to conceal the raw edges leaving 1.5 cm (⅝ in) showing on both sides. Slip stitch into the stitching line.

Edgings

Tablecloths which fall simply and straight to the ground always look so forlorn when compared to a heavily padded cloth made long enough to drape on to the floor. Binding the lower edge or adding a chunky cord will add weight to help the draped folds sit well on the floor. Corded edges can be added to lengthen a cloth which is a touch too short, or to disguise a worn or marked edge.

Hem Finishes

A tablecloth which has no weight falls straight to the floor in limp folds. Adding interlining and lining improves the body of the fabric. Extending the length of the drop so that the folds of the cloth fall outwards and catch on the floor, also improves the drape. But more weight is needed if the cloth is to stay draped on its own. Bought trimmings, such as a heavy cord, allow the fabric to be moulded into shape, while a bullion or tasselled fringe will catch on the floor and pull the folds out. A frill performs the same function, but is too feminine for many situations; an attached roll allows the cloth to be positioned in wide scallops; an applied border adds weight discreetly.

1. A padded, quilted border adds weight and helps the cloth to hang and pleat neatly. Made from the same fabric, the border is quite discreet, the only detail being the piping at the top and bottom in a closely related colour. Vary the look by combining other colours. Try terracotta fabric bordered in black with blue/green piping. Or experiment with natural linen which would look effective with a dusty pink floral border, piped in soft pink.
2. Frilled hems are eminently suited to more feminine bedrooms and bathrooms. This deep frill catches on the floor and helps to hold the folds away from the table. Stitch the frill so that the bottom is approximately 1 cm (½ in) longer than the cloth behind it. A short frill stitched

along the hemline can be attractive in a child's room or a cottage-style guest bedroom, whereas a very deep, piped frill could be added to heavier damask and velvet cloths. Allow a minimum of one-and-a-half times fullness and a maximum of three times. Be prepared to use a lot of fabric, as even on a small table (say 60 cm/24 in high and wide), twice the circumference measurement of the tablecloth is over 11 metres (13 yards).
3. A jumbo cord in two-tone green and cream adds weight and tradition to a lined tablecloth. It

also adds an extra colour dimension and provides a neat finishing touch.
4. Perhaps the simplest of finishes – layers of cloths in pretty provençal prints and large checks create several 'hems' or borders; the top cloth anchors the ones beneath in place.
5. A rich, crewel embroidered overcloth has been given a smart finishing touch with an attractive edging of two-colour fringing. Braid or fringing can also be used to make a too-short cloth that little bit longer and to add weight to any fabric.

LAMPSHADES

Lampshades can be accent points (in the same way that a scarlet bow might set off a black and white evening dress) or they can add a subtle dimension to your living room. Pleated fabric or card shades in tones of oyster, cream, ivory and buttermilk always deserve consideration for the amount of warm, diffused, relaxed light they give. The quality of the light thrown by gathered shades will depend on the fabric you choose: very soft, floaty silks or fine linens will just filter it to give a soft glow, while a heavier chintz or calico will obscure the light, throwing it downwards to create pools on the surface below. Before making a final decision, hold the fabric over the frame to see how much light passes through and check to see whether it creases.

PLEATED FABRIC SHADES

For elegant pleated fabric shades bind the top and bottom of the shade as on page 185. Pleat around either the top or bottom ring if it is empire or drum in shape. With a coolie shade the fabric is pleated and overlapped around the top and only slightly gathered around the base; cut and join enough fabric to cover the bottom ring one-and-a-half to two times. For an empire frame, allow three times the top or bottom ring circumference. Cut each strip 4 cm (1½ in) longer than the shade depth, measuring along the slope.

Lampshade stitch

Make a double vertical stitch about 3 mm (⅛ in) deep, bringing the thread out at the top. Take the thread down diagonally about 1 cm (⅜ in). Make another vertical double stitch. Repeat; adjust each stitch to suit the frame and catch pleats in place.

---

1. To line the shade, estimate the amount of lining fabric needed by placing the frame on its side and marking the top and bottom of one of the struts. Roll the shade through 360°, running a pencil line around the lower edge as you go. Over-cut this piece by 6 cm (2¼ in) in all directions.

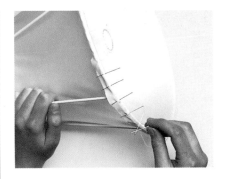

2. Drape the fabric around the outside of the shade, pinning along the seam and attaching it into the top and bottom rings. Pin and re-pin until the fabric is taut and all the wrinkles have been removed.

3. Trim to within 2 cm (¾ in) of the frame. Remove and stitch the seam from the wrong side, using a very narrow zig-zag stitch. The lining may be attached to the frame either now, or after the pleated top cover has been stitched to the frame. Pin back on to the frame – this time from the inside, again re-pinning until the lining is taut.

4. Stitch all around with lampshade stitch. Stitch at the front of the rings. Trim the lining close to the stitching line.

5. Place one width of the fabric on to the worktable and pleat up one long side, taking 3 cm (1¼ in) for each 1 cm (¾ in) of pleat. Pin to the top of the frame, keeping the pleats straight and even. Do not make machined joins – just overlap the next piece, incorporating the selvedges into the next pleat. Stitch each pleat in place, catching down each fold.

6. Attach the fabric to the bottom ring, keeping the pleats straight and evenly spaced between the frame struts. Gather evenly and pin at very close intervals so that each gather looks like a tiny pleat. Stitch in place. Trim away any excess.

7. Make small rolls of lining fabric to loop around the two frame joints on the top ring, so hiding the raw lining edge. Stitch to the frame and trim excess.

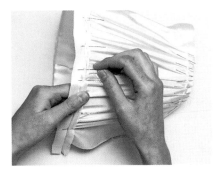

8. To bind the edge, cut a strip of fabric 4 cm (1½ in) wide, the length of the ring circumference. Press into three. Open out and pin around the ring so that 1 cm (⅜ in) is above and the rest below.

9. Stitch in place with lampshade stitch. Join the two ends on the diagonal. Fold the binding back on itself to cover all raw edges.

INFORMAL SHADES

Gathered shades are very simple to make and take a small amount of fabric – offcuts of furnishings fabric, the smallest piece of a favourite, extravagant fabric or simple cotton lawn can be usefully regenerated. Gathered covers need a metal or card frame beneath to hold the shape, and are usually fitted over an existing card shade, either to soften the light, to add a more feminine touch to the room, or to cover up a worn shade beneath.

MAKING UP

Measure the depth and circumference of the under shade. Allow 3-6 cm (1¼–2¼ in) to fall below the bottom of the frame and for fullness estimate one-and-a-half times the circumference. Add approximately 8-12 cm (3¼–4¾ in) for a frilled heading, or double the finished frill size plus 2 cm (¾ in) for gathering. But remember, the more fullness in the shade, the less light will be able to penetrate. Cut and join the fabric as necessary to make a full circle.

Golden toile de jouy throws a warm light and full gathers soften the direct beam, concentrating light downwards for reading. The scalloped picot edge is a pretty touch.

1. Make a template for the scalloped edge. Mark a piece of card into equal sections of between 8 and 12 cm (3¼ and 4¾ in) and then make curves within each one by drawing around a household object, e.g., a glass, a saucer or a pot lid.

2. Cut out the fabric using the template. Pin the picot edging around, 1.5 cm (⅝ in) from the edge, following the shapes of the curves and especially keeping the points sharp – the definition can easily be lost at this stage. Stitch the picot edge in place.

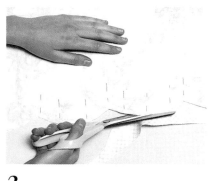

3. Pin the top fabric to the lining, right sides facing and stitch together, following the last stitching line.

Trim the fabric to shape, snipping right into the points. Turn to the right side and press the scalloped edge neatly.

4. Measure the length of the shade from the hem upwards, including the frilled heading allowance. Fold the rest to the back. Neaten both fabrics as necessary and press the raw edge under. Stitch around, close to this fold, leaving a 2 cm (¾ in) opening next to the seam. Stitch round again 1.5 cm (⅝ in) above. Thread a ribbon through this channel and tie up when the cover sits comfortably over the under shade.

PLEATED CARD SHADES

Pleated card shades are, to the relief of some, absolutely no-sew shades. Taking little fabric and time, one large or two small shades can realistically be accomplished in one evening.

You will need the top ring only for smaller shades and a frame with top and bottom rings for anything over 30 cm (12 in) across the bottom. Make sure that the fitting you buy will suit the purpose – if you have a shade carrier a single ring is enough, for a ceiling light you will need the complete gimbal fitting.

I prefer the look of fabric on pleated shades but wallpapers and decorative papers could be substituted. If you can't find the adhesive backing used here, make your own by pasting a medium weight card to the back of your fabric or paper.

MAKING UP

Measure the metal frame or an existing shade to decide the depth needed. For the depth, the fabric should extend approximately 5 cm (2 in) below the frame. For the length, you will need two to three times the finished circumference depending how small and full you want the pleats to be. It is best to test the effect of some different sized pleats with a piece of stiff paper before you start.

You will need a right angle and a metal straight edge to complete this lampshade.

Concertina pleats make an interesting variation on the rigid lines of formal checks.

DESIGN AND MAKE SOFT FURNISHINGS

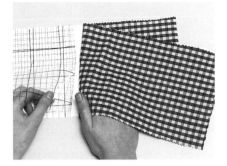

1. Cut your length of fabric and finish with pinking sheers if you have them. If not, cut the edges as cleanly as possible and avoid handling the fabric. If you have chosen a fabric which frays greatly, press the fabric on to the finest fusible interfacing you can find before you cut it. Cut the backing material to the exact size. Place the fabric over, so that as the adhesive side is unrolled you can press the fabric down with the palm of your hand, smoothing out any creases and air bubbles.

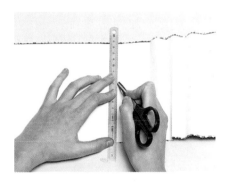

2. Trim away any excess fabric. With the aid of a metal straight edge, mark out each pleat. Use a right angle frequently to make sure that the pleats do not start to lean. Pleat up in concertina style.

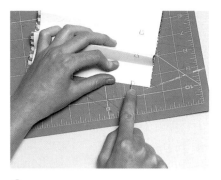

3. You will need to make a hole for the ring to pass through and it is possible to use a paper punch. However to obtain the best fit, inverted V shapes need to be cut at the inner edge of each pleat. Again test on a spare piece of paper to determine the best size, but you should just be able to press the ring in and the paper cut should close over it.

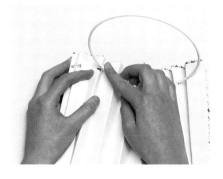

4. Press the ring into each cut and concertina the pleats together tightly. Join the ends with PVA adhesive and hold together until set. Clamp large paper clips to the top and bottom to hold the shade securely overnight.

5. Thread ribbon through at the front and tie into a bow. If the ring does show through between the pleats, you can either paint the frame to match or tone with the fabric, or wind ribbon around the ring between each pleat.

Small, candle-sized shades are a treat to make, being easy to handle and immediately rewarding. The brass ring at the top adds an attractive dimension; here it is fitted to a candle holder but it can also serve as a bulb clip for an electric light.

DINING ROOMS AND KITCHENS

Simple checks are ideal for a farmhouse kitchen. These come from a hotel supplier and have been manufactured specifically for hard wear and frequent laundering.

In many homes today, meals in the dining room are reserved for occasions like Christmas and Easter and celebrations like birthdays and anniversaries. For this reason, both settings and furnishings often tend to be traditional: damask or linen tablecloths, matching or contrasting napkins and upholstered or slip covered chairs.

On the whole, though, life is less formal and many of us now entertain much more in the kitchen – morning coffee, a glass of wine after work or family suppers – and furnishings and settings reflect this. A good selection of tablecloths supplies the basis for interesting table decorations; and checks, stripes, florals, small stylised prints and neat provençal prints combine together successfully, mixing and matching and providing an adaptable base for a number of occasions. Choose colours of the same tonal range for uncomplicated harmony, and finish the cloths by hemming the sides using contrasting coloured threads. Plain coloured ribbon, braid or tape make a good finish for the edges of a patterned cloth.

Kitchen chairs are not always comfortable to sit on for any length of time and some sort of comfortable seat pad becomes essential. Squab cushions (see page 116) are flat pieces of foam or stitched hair, made to fit the seat shape, covered in fabric and tied to the legs at the back of the chair.

DESIGN AND MAKE SOFT FURNISHINGS

TABLE LINEN

Tablecloths can be made from crisp white linen or cotton damask for use in dining rooms, or they can be altogether more interchangeable and relaxed for kitchen meals, like the layered ones above. Placemats and napkins add essential accents to settings. Square or rectangular tablecloths are the easiest to make and also fit circular tables. Measure the top of the table, push a dining chair in place, then measure from the table edge to the seat. Add this to each side of the tabletop measurements: usually 15–20 cm (6–8 in) for a kitchen table, slightly more for a dining one. Allow 3 cm (1¼ in) all round for hem allowances and make up in the usual way.

DESIGN AND MAKE SOFT FURNISHINGS

Ideas for Corners

Decorating the table can be as much fun as preparing the meal and choosing the crockery. I often use plain cloths, decorating the centre with fresh, expendable greenery, from the garden – a few lengths of green creeper placed across a white tablecloth can look effortlessly dramatic against glass or silver. I like to tie plain, white napkins with fronds of honeysuckle or wisteria and push a daisy or rose into the top.

A patterned cloth provides its own decoration. Calico or linen can make inexpensive cloths but sometimes you might like to embellish the corners.

1. Use a button to hold folds of fabric in gentle cascades. Cover the button in fabric, or choose leather, metal, an elaborate bejewelled creation, or children's motifs, such as teddies, boats or frogs for a birthday party.

2. A simple bow makes a more elaborate decoration, perhaps for a wedding or anniversary. Lengths of fabric to match or contrast, ribbons or cotton tapes – experiment with pinking the edges, or cut gingham on the cross and gently fray the sides.

3. Extravagant loops of satin, petersham or florist's ribbon and a dried hydrangea provide the decoration for an autumn supper. Replace the dried flower with fresh for a summer party. Bind the stem with damp cotton wool to preserve blooms.

Placemats

Whatever the cloth or table surface beneath, once the table is prepared, it is the place setting which takes the attention. How much more inviting and special is a bowl of homemade soup when presented on an interesting, colourful placemat.

Try to buy quilted fabric but if you can't find anything you really like, then quilt your own before making up. To find the best size for you, lay a full table setting and practise with paper placemats until you have determined the perfect size. An interesting, complementary lining makes all the difference, but choose one with the same washing requirements.

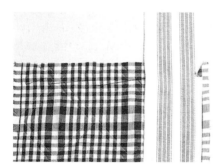

1. Cut the placemat to size, centring any pattern, stripe or check. Cut a length of contrast fabric the circumference of the placemat and 8 cm (3¼ in) wide for a 2.5 cm (1 in) finished edge. Pin the binding to the right side, setting the edge 1 cm (⅜ in) from the placemat edge. Stop 2.5 cm (1 in) from the corner.

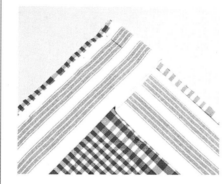

2. Fold the binding edge back at an exact 45° angle and continue to pin along the adjacent side. Repeat with the next and following corners. Join the two ends of the binding neatly.

3. Press the seam flat and stitch the binding to the mat, exactly 1.5 cm (⅝ in) from the edge. Stop at each corner and secure. Start again on the other side of the flap, inserting the needle right against the last stitch.

4. Press the binding from the right side, away from the mat. Mitre each corner (see page 8) and fold the sides under.

5. Mitre the corners on the wrong side and turn under 1.5 cm (⅝ in) to conceal the raw edges. Slip stitch along the fold, to the stitching line. Use small stitches to prevent gaping and to make the stitching line as strong as possible.

Napkins

Colourful napkins provide the finishing touch to kitchen supper. Choose fabrics which will wash well and require minimum ironing. Checked fabrics are readily available and contrast well with so many other patterns or plain colours.

Lunch napkins should be at least 35 cm (14 in) square. As most fabrics are 130-135 cm (52-54 in) wide, three napkins can be cut across each width of fabric. Dinner napkins should be at least 50 cm (20 in) square, so are not as economical to cut. Always allow 3 cm (1¼ in) all around and finish with a machine or extremely tiny hand stitches.

A simple hem is all that is needed for a patterned fabric and any extraneous detail can be avoided if you have chosen an eclectic mix of colours and patterns. A classic choice of blue/white with yellow/white might look good with some

contrasting stitching. Perhaps a sharp blue edge, satin-stitched around a yellow/white napkin lying on a blue and white cloth with a yellow stitched edge.

Fray the edges for a country look. Stitch a small zig zag line approximately 3 cm (1¼ in) from the edge of each napkin. Pin the napkin to a flat surface and pull the threads one at a time from one side at a time. If the edges bind together with washing, just comb them out lightly.

Napkins are so simple to make, that there is really no excuse for not running up six or eight in matching or complementary sets. If you are making a tablecloth anyway, plan to sew napkins as well. Or make several sets, tie with ribbon or cord and present as attractive gifts.

CHAIRS

Often side chairs and carvers have backs and arms which interrupt the flow of a skirt. The only solution is to make as many skirt sections as needed, with flaps at each end to button over each other. Neat and precise cutting and finishing is essential for a pleasing result, so should only be tackled by an experienced sewer.

On the chair on the left, as in many others, the back of the chair has been designed and made to join the seat. The back skirt panel has to be made as a completely separate piece, held only by the rows of buttons at each side.

Top right: A remnant showing ladies in Provençe National Costume was not quite large enough to cover this side chair. The solution was to seam it with a jolly red and white check around the frill. Long ties laced around the back legs keep the cover securely in place.

Bottom right: Simple, bib-like covers can be quickly made and easily removed for laundering. Make a template of the chair seat and add 12 cm (4¾ in) all around. At the back corner keep the cut-outs, using these to make the flaps which button around the legs. Hem or line the cover. Tack a cord around to hold the 'bib' in place and knot at the front corners to gather up excess fabric.

MAKING UP

To make loose covers for a set of upholstered dining chairs or a single desk chair, first measure, plan and cut fabric pieces as shown on pages 182–83. You will need to decide your preferred skirt style and then follow the instructions and ideas on pages 28–29 to make up. You will also need to make up enough piping to finish the whole chair.

The basic principles are the same as for an upholstered armchair or sofa, so read these through carefully before starting and refer to them as necessary (see pages 19–20 and 22–23).

1. Pin the inner and outer back pieces to the chair, placing the fabric centre fold against the pinned centre line of the chair and keeping the grain straight. Anchor to the outer edge all around. Pin these two pieces together following the back line tight to the chair back.

2. Make a dart at the top corners and ease any fullness from the front curve. Fit so that the pins are lying nose to tail and the fabric is completely pucker free. Cut the seat piece and place over. Pin the two pieces together as shown, marking the side seams and cutting an amount for the 'tuck-in' between seat and back.

3. Trim all excess fabric back to 2 cm (¾ in) and make V cuts to assist you in matching the two pieces once the pins have been removed. Mark the seam around the seat with coloured marking tacks to match it up again easily.

4. For a skirt starting at the seat's bottom, make front darts, and trim fabric to 2 cm (¾ in) below the frame.

5. If your skirt is to start from the seat line, then pencil around seat edge and cut to shape with a 2 cm (¾ in) seam allowance. Measure from seam line at top of seat, or the bottom of the upholstery to the floor, to find finished skirt length.

6. Remove pinned cover. Make any darts at the top corners and the seat front. Join seam between the inner back and seat. Pin piping around outer back and stitch, snipping to ease around shaping and to make a sharp corner.

7. Pin inner back to outer back, easing as needed, and stitch inside the piping stitching line. Check right side to see if first stitching line shows. If it does, stitch around again close to piping, until piping is neat and even. Pipe around seat if not already piped. Neaten seams.

Dining chair backs are seen as much as fronts around a table. The scope for decoration is limited only by time and fabric choice.

DINING ROOMS AND KITCHENS: CHAIRS 57

CREATING A DINING SET

Once you have cut the first pattern and completed your first covers, you might be inspired to make more sets for other occasions.

Instead of making up a separate frilled skirt, add 18 cm (7 in) to the outer back length and around the three sides of the seat template. A stencilled design can be painted on to each piece before stitching together. Use fabric paints, dry and press under a clean cloth with a hot iron. A simple hem was stitched all around and the back openings stitched together. Fabric-covered buttons stencilled with a miniature grape design hold small pleats at both legs.

For a tailored fit (above), the back was cut into three panels, shaped to take up the fullness. The two pleats were created by leaving the back seams open beyond the seat. Pretty stencilled fabric buttons define the pleats and punctuate the plain cream.

To make a back opening (right), the outer back template is cut through the centre and 8 cm (3¼ in) added to both sides. Instead of the frilled skirt, add 18 cm (7 in) to the length. Also add 18 cm (7 in) to three sides of the seat template. Make up the outer back first. Press extra fabric under, 2 cm (¾ in) from centre back line. Neaten raw edges. Pin together two layers, lining up centres and overlapping by 4 cm (1½ in). Make buttonholes on top piece and stitch covered button-holes on under piece.

Make up the cover as before, stitching the backs to the hem.

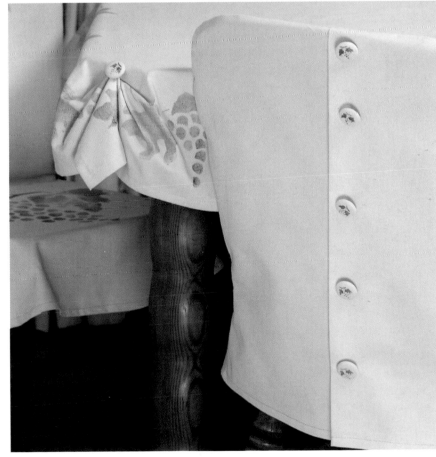

KITCHEN CHAIRS

A set of slip-over covers for kitchen chairs like those shown on page 49 can be made in a day. See pages 182–83 for fabric quantities.

You will find that wood-framed chairs need to be bound with lengths of fabric to provide an anchor for pinning.

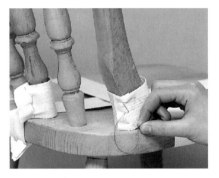

1. Stitch tapes tightly in place to stop swivelling as pinned fabrics pull against each other. Drawing pins can hold tapes on old frames. Sticky tape can be used, but may remove paint.

2. For a seat template, pin some calico to the taped edges. Push a pencil into the fabric around the back legs and cut calico to shape. Pencil around chair seat's edge and cut fabric along line. Check that the template is fixed and follows the seat shape. Put a note on the calico to add seam allowances.

3. Cutting the back is a little more difficult if you have not made enough pinning points. (This cover should fall loosely, but the template cover must fit quite tightly.) The front and back pieces at the top of the chair must be pinned together close to the frame and the fabric at each side must be equal. Trim seams to 2 cm (¾ in) and make notches and marking tacks to assist you when stitching pieces together – always mark any easement. Cut around the seat without seam allowances, but cut a 2 cm (¾ in) seam allowance for the back and front piece – note it in pencil on the template.

4. Cut out fabric pieces for the inner back, outer back, seat skirt and two plackets. Add seam allowances where necessary. This skirt was cut 20 cm (8 in) long to allow 4 cm (1½ in) for the hem and 2 cm (¾ in) for the seam allowance. Make up flat piping. Cut fabric strips on the cross 5 cm (2 in) wide and press in half.

5. Stitch the inner back to the seat and neaten the seam. Pin flat piping to the outer back all around, making small tucks at the top corners and stitch in place. Pin the inner back to the stitching line and ease or pleat the fullness around the top. Stitch flat piping around the seat and along the hemline of the outer back. To make up the skirts, make 2 cm (¾ in) double hems to finish. Stitch gathering threads along the top, pull up and pin to the seat and back, distributing the gathers evenly.

6. Make ties (see page 8) – four or six for each side. Pin one 3 cm (1⅛ in) below the top opening, one at the top of the skirt and one in between if needed. Make a placket (see page 10) and pin over the ties. As you stitch the placket in place, triple stitch backwards and forwards over the ties to hold them securely in place.

The seam joining the seat to the inner back should fit snugly to the wood. Flat piping, cut on the cross, between the seat and the skirt makes an attractive finish.

A placket stitched around the back opening encloses all raw edges and secures the fabric ties.

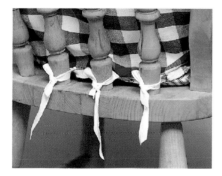

Long tapes need to be stitched to the inner back/seat seam and tied to each chair back strut to prevent the seat moving. You can just see the ticking squab which sits on the seat, under the loose cover.

This simple cover reminds me of a horse blanket – reversible, easy to store when not in use and very simple to make. Place the seat template on to the fabric and cut around the back with no allowance for seams. Add 12 cm (5 in) to the sides and front, following the curves and shape of the template. Stitch petersham ribbon or bias binding all around and make ties for the back legs to secure the cover to the seat.

BEDROOMS

A new look for the most traditional fabrics — denim, gingham, tartan, Normandy stripes and Madras checks: ostensibly for a teenage bedroom, but who would not be comfortable sleeping here?

The master bedroom is probably – in living terms – the most important room in the house after the kitchen and the family room, and the bed itself will always be the main piece of furniture. For this reason, its furnishings can make or break the overall design of the room. Matching headboards – slip covered or tied – and valances will create a harmonious effect and, what's more, a valance can conceal a host of unattractive items from under-bed springs to a well-worn divan base. For both, choose a fabric that works with your overall scheme but especially with your bedcovers. These can be throwovers, fitted or duvets, but whatever type you choose remember that it will set the tone for the rest of the room. Pillows and bolsters add a welcoming finishing touch.

Historically, the main bedroom was always granted great status - as can be seen in the many chateaux and country houses which open their rooms to the public - and beds were hung with curtains such as the corona, which is fitted centrally above the bed from the ceiling, or on the back wall, central to the width of the bed. Bed curtains can be unlined, lined or interlined and are increasingly fashionable today. This chapter includes these and half tester curtains as well as a canopy and a corona.

There are also suggestions for fabric-covered dressing tables and some ideas for solving the ever-present problem of storage.

HEADBOARD COVERS

Design a cover for a headboard to suit whatever style of bed or bedroom you have to work with. With a little imagination and following the instructions given, you can adapt these ideas to design your own, either a slip cover or a tied one.

Use a quilted fabric for a slip cover if your headboard is a little flat, and also for one which is padded and buttoned as the quilting will prevent the fabric from following the contours and dipping into the buttoned recesses.

As long as the basic shape is good, any unfashionable wooden headboard can be given a new lease of life with a slip cover. Firstly, re-upholster the wooden board with fire retardent foam and calico to give you a soft and comfortable back to sit against.

If you wish to make a new bed head, first cut a paper template and pin to the wall behind the bed to check the shape. Consider the pictures you might want to hang above, whether you want to have a canopy and what shape this will be, how many pillows you will need and how high.

Piping the edge of a headboard cover helps to identify the line, especially if the shape is quite intricate. Piping should be bold enough to define the edge but not so strong as to overpower the pattern of the fabric. A deep tone picked up from the main fabric gives definition to a print.

Long ties are another alternative for a shaped headboard (above), as they can be adjusted along the length of the cover.

This vibrant print in gold and red, depicting the story of the discovery of America, has been used for the bedcover as well as the headboard and is a firm contrast to the plain cotton pillow cases.

Your bed head should finish on the divan, below the mattress and be approximately 3 cm (1¼ in) wider than the width of the bed. Use foam approximately 4 cm (1½ in) deep and position the foam so that it starts at the top of the mattress; any lower and it will not fit correctly but instead will push the mattress forwards.

Cut the foam to shape and glue to the wood with a PVA glue. Staple all around approximately 3 mm (⅛ in) from the edge of the foam, making a neat rounded edge. Stretch calico over the front, staple to the back of the board and make a back lining also with calico. Pull the calico tight for wrinkle-free corners.

Tied sides look very attractive (below), especially when made from a contrast fabric, ribbon or a check or striped fabric cut on the cross. But ties do not always need to be functional: make up a bordered headboard and stitch purely decorative ties or ribbons opposite each other into the piping seams. Tie in generous floppy bows or small, neat ties.

This cover (above) consists only of two pieces of lined fabric, one for the front and one for the back, shaped exactly as the wooden board, lined and with eyelets inset at intervals all around the top. Self ties thread though from front to back and tie in bold loops. Unlike the picture on the right, these ties are essential to hold the cover in place. Buttons and tabs, button-holes and toggles or button-holes and cufflinks could have been used instead for an individual touch.

To add some interest to an all white scheme, I used a picot edging in cream instead of piping (right). A flap in matching white damask edged with the same creamy picot lace is fastened down with pearl buttons. Cushions and pillows in cream and white silks, cottons and organdies emphasise the 'elegant romantic' style.

Tied Headboard Covers

MAKING UP

Measure the widest and highest points of the headboard to estimate the fabric cuts needed for the back and front pieces. A single headboard will usually fit into one width of fabric, but larger ones will need to have widths seamed together. Join pieces to either side of the centre panel to avoid centre seams.

1. Measure all around the headboard to determine the length needed for the gusset – from the base on one side up and over the top to the base on the other side, then add 6 cm (2¼ in) for turnings and 2 cm (¾ in) either side of the board width for the seam allowances. Cut the gusset out across the fabric width and join as necessary, again keeping a full width for the centre and joining a piece to either side.

2. Cut out the binding and ties. Fold the remaining fabric in half across the width so that the fold follows a 45 degree line to the checks. Cut 12 pieces 45 × 6 cm (18 × 2¼ in) for the ties and two pieces the same length as the gusset × 7 cm (3 in) wide for the binding. Press the bindings in half lengthways and pin. To make the ties, follow the instructions on page 8, turn one end in and stitch along the fold lines.

3. Measure carefully across the bottom and top of the headboard and mark the centres with pins. Make a line of pins from top to bottom on back and front to mark the centre lines. Fold the front fabric in half with the right sides together and finger press the centre fold. Position on to the headboard, lining up the centre fold to the pinned line. Unfold the top piece gradually and anchor the fabric to the headboard, pinning along the centre line and at approximately 15 cm (6 in) intervals all around the outside edge. Repeat with the back piece.

4. Pin the gusset around the headboard, lining it up at the centre top to match the back and front pieces. Holding the fabric firmly between finger and thumb, pin the front and back pieces to the gusset, starting at the centre top and pinning towards each side at approximately 20 cm (8 in) intervals. Pin back into these spaces, so that the pins will run nose to tail all the way along the top of the headboard. This pin line will be the stitching line, so must be accurate. Ease any fullness carefully into tiny gathers so that the front fabric does not pull. Pin down both sides.

5. Trim away the excess fabric to leave a 2 cm (¾ in) seam allowance. Snip balance marks at intervals around the cover. (These will be used to match back to front when the pins have been removed, so are vital to the success of the final cover.)

6. When you are happy with the fit of the cover, remove first the anchor pins and then the complete cover. Take out the pins holding the gusset to the cover front. Pin the other binding strip around the cover, lining up the raw edge of the binding with the trimmed edge of the cover exactly. Snip into the binding if necessary for ease and stitch together 2 cm (¾ in) in. Pin the other strip of binding to the back of the gusset strip and stitch with the same 2 cm (¾ in) seam allowance.

7. Position three ties on either side of the cover front, with the first one approximately 12 cm (5 in) from the top and the other two with approximately 20 cm (8 in) gaps. Pin the front of the gusset to the cover front, and stitch together just inside the first stitching line, securing each tie firmly with a reverse stitch.

8. Position the other six ties on to the gusset exactly opposite each stitched tie. Pin the back piece to the gusset, following the notches through from the front to make sure that the fronts and backs are fully matched, and stitch in place.

9. Fit the cover on to the headboard, trim any excess fabric and pin the hem line. Remove the cover, fold the fabric under double to make a hem and stitch. Make eight ties and stitch to both sides at intervals of approximately 30 cm (12 in) to tie under the headboard to keep the cover in place. Press and sleeve back on to the headboard. Finger press all seam allowances in the same direction and tie at the lower edge.

When asked to re-design a guest bedroom, my only brief was that all furnishings should be easy to launder, should stand the test of time and be equally suitable for male or female, child or adult.

White bed linen was chosen both for its appearance and practicality. For the headboard and chair covers this large scale red gingham proved to be the perfect partner to the rough walls and white tones, adding fresh colour but remaining within the simplistic tenor of the country situation.

VALANCES

Bed valances are generally pleated, gathered or straight, with any number of added variations including false pleats to give access to divan drawers.

However they are designed they should be lined and full enough to give body.

MAKING UP

Measure the bed base from the top to the floor. Note any unusual projections, bedposts etc, which might prevent the valance fitting easily, especially on old beds and four posters. Measure the length and width of the bed base (the platform), then the position of any bedhead fixings. Make a template of the corners at both the top and bottom ends of the bed base. Decide how long you want the valance to be and how full. I always allow three times fullness depending on the weight of the fabric. Allow at least 1 cm (³⁄₈ in) for a frilled skirt to drape to the floor. Plan the widths of fabric needed. Allow seam allowances – 2 cm (³⁄₄ in) all around the platform and 6 cm (2¼ in) for the skirt.

1. Cut the skirt widths of the main fabric and lining; join. Press the seams flat. Make three strips of fabric 15 cm (6 in) wide, two the length of the bed and one the width. Cut and join lining to make the platform, the width and length of the bed plus 2 cm (³⁄₄ in) seam allowance all around.

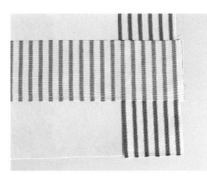

2. Press under 1.5 cm (⁵⁄₈ in) all along one side of each of the strips for the platform border. Pin all three pieces on to the platform. Fold the side pieces back at the corners to mitre the joins. Stitch all around the inside of these strips.

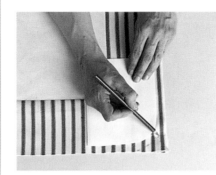

3. Place the corner template on to the platform, add the seam allowance and cut round.

4. Pin piping all around the three sides and 15 cm (6 in) around the top corners along the bedhead.

5. Stitch the skirt lining to the main fabric, right sides together, with a 1.5 cm (⁵⁄₈ in) seam allowance. Press from the front, pressing the fabric towards the lining. Turn over and press from the back, folding along the fabric to show 2–2.5 cm (³⁄₄–1 in).

6. Pin all along the top edge and trim the lining to match the main fabric exactly. Press the fabric and lining ends in and slipstitch together. Stitch a double gathering thread all around 1.5 cm (⁵⁄₈ in) and 2 cm (³⁄₄ in) from the top.

7. Divide the valance into 10 equal sections and mark each with coloured tacks. Mark the three sides of the platform into 10 equal sections. Pin the skirt to the platform, matching these points. Pull the threads to gather each section and pin the gathering line to the piping line.

8. Stitch all around. Neaten the seam and press. Stitch tape into each corner so that you can secure the valance to each bed leg. Lift the mattress from the bed. Place the valance on top of the bed base and tie the tapes around the legs.

1

6

2

3

4

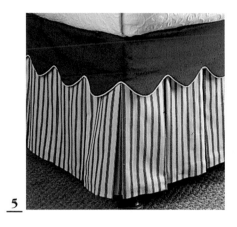

5

Edgings and Finishes

1. For a pretty country finish, cut the valance a little shorter than floor length to allow a picot lace or broderie anglais trim. The edge was first piped with 20 mm (¾ in) ribbon in the deeper blue, and the lining slip stitched over to cover the raw edges. This style of valance looks good cut 10–15 cm (4–6 in) short for antique brass or iron frame beds.

2. Binding the hem adds an attractive detail but also weights the skirt, allowing it to fall well whether it drapes on to the floor or hangs short. Cut 6 cm (2¼ in) strips on the cross for checks or stripes, but on the straight for plain fabrics. Stitch right sides together along the hemline, 1.4 cm (just under ⅝ in) from the raw edges. Press binding to the back leaving a neat 1.5 cm (⅝ in) edge. Fold the raw edge under and slipstitch to the stitching line. If the valance is lined, tack stitch the lining and main fabric together before adding the binding.

3. Double valances are always interesting – use stripes or checks cut on the cross, two patterned fabrics with similar colour tones or two contrasting plain fabrics. Two separate valances are made up and joined together with the gathering thread. To reduce bulk, the under-valance is made from a single layer, cut to floor length, with just a border of main fabric added to the front. Cut the border to the chosen depth, adding 10 cm (4 in) for turnings. Stitch the right side of the border to the wrong side of the lining hem, press to the front, press the raw edge under 1 cm (⅜ in) and stitch to the under-valance, close to the fold line.

4. Pipe or bind one or both of the valances with contrasting fabric.

5. Allow three times fullness for box-pleated valances and pleat up so that they open at each corner. The flat scalloped top was made up, piped, lined and stitched to the pleated valance along the top before joining to the piped edge of the valance platform.

6. Stitch any closely woven, preshrunk ribbon or braid to the main fabric before making up. Place the ribbon carefully, considering the depth of valance, the depth of the ribbon and the bedcovers which will be used.

BED CURTAINS

Once necessary to keep out the cold and 'harmful' night air, bed curtains are now used to create atmosphere in a bedroom.

Unlined Curtains

These are effective when plenty of fabric is used to create softness and body. But remember, the fabric must look as good from inside as from outside.

MAKING UP

To make four curtains, one for each corner which will pull to close, use at least two widths of fabric for each curtain and three to four widths for sheer fabrics.

1. Cut and join lengths, allowing 8 cm (3¼ in) turnings for the heading and 4 cm (1½ in) for the hem. Lightweight curtains should be overlong, and don't forget to allow the draping allowance if the curtains are to be tied up. Use flat seams and press thoroughly.

2. Working with one curtain at a time, press 4 cm (1½ in) to the wrong side of each side and hem. Press in half and fold under to make 2 cm (¾ in) turnings. Mitre the bottom corners, stitch with a decorative machine stitch or slip stitch by hand along the fold; press.

3. Place the curtain on to the worktable and press flat. Measure from the hem to the heading and mark the overall drop. Mark 8 cm (3¼ in) above this line and trim away any excess. Press the 8 cm (3¼ in) allowance to the wrong side. Press in half to make a 4 cm (1⅝ in) turning. Pin all along.

4. For a simple heading, cut ribbons or tapes to the required length. Fold in half and pin under the fold line at regular intervals the length of the heading. Stitch close to the fold line, carefully double stitching over the ribbons or tapes to secure and stitch another row 5 mm (¼ in) from the overall drop line.

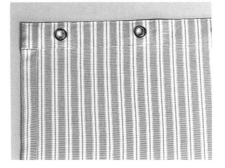

5. If you are using eyelets, make holes and fit the eyelets at regular intervals along the top once all the stitching is complete.

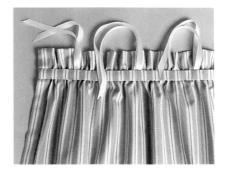

6. To disguise the back of the gathering tape, cut a band of main fabric, fold under the raw edges and slip stitch in place.

HEADINGS

If the curtains are to hang from a metal rail they will need to look as good inside as outside.

Insert a piece of 5 cm (2 in) buckram between the interlining and the inner curtain. Herringbone to the interlining. Fold both fabrics in and slip stitch together to match the sides.

If the curtains are being fitted beneath a pelmet or behind a corona, the hooks will be fitted from the front, as the inside of the bed hangings will be seen. Either gather by hand or use bought heading tapes. Fold both fabrics to the front and stitch whichever heading tape you choose to use, approximately 2 cm (¾ in) from the top. Pull up threads or gather by hand.

Unlined curtains made from beige and white ticking are fastened to the metal frame with ties made from curtain heading tape. Overlong curtains bunch into extravagant drapes at each corner.

Lined Bed Curtains

Lining bed curtains offers a lovely chance to make the inside of the bed a completely different character to the outside. In the room here, outside the bed is completely white with a deep blue border around; inside the furnishings are all blue and white.

MAKING UP

1. Cut and join curtain lengths, allowing at least two widths of fabric in each curtain. Add 10 cm (4 in) for the hems and headings.

Blue and white stripes line white towelling fabric for a fresh summer bedroom (left). Deep blue edgings, tablecloth and cushions bring weight of colour to balance the polished, deep mahogany bed head. A pretty toile de jouy bedcover tells the story of the first hot air balloon flight.

Light cottons take on a completely new form and character when thick interlining is sandwiched between the layers. Coordinated Provençal fabrics in rich ochre and forest green have been used in the room on the right for both outer and inner curtains.

2. Place the curtain front on to the worktable, right sides facing down. Lay the lining fabric over and lock stitch together along the seam. Press both fabrics together and pin at 10 cm (4 in) intervals all around the outside edges. Trim away any excess so that all four sides are equal.

3. Cut strips of fabric for the binding, 8 cm (3¾ in) wide for a 2 cm (¾ in) edging, and join to make one long length. Turn the curtain over carefully and pin the edging strips on, mitring the corners.

Machine stitch 1.9 cm (just under ¾ in) from the raw edges. Stop at the corner mitre and fasten off with double stitches. Fold the flap of fabric over and re-start on the opposite side.

4. Press the binding strips to the front, mitre the corners, and fold to the underside, leaving an accurate 2 cm (¾ in) edging. From the back, press the binding under and pin to secure. Slip stitch to the stitching line with tiny stitches.

5. Finish the heading by stitching ties, making pleats or inserting eyelets as described on page 70.

Interlined Curtains

1. Join the widths of fabric which you have allowed for each curtain. Trim away selvages and any writing. Snip into the seam allowance if the fabric feels tight; press. Join the interlining and lining and press the seams flat.

2. Place the main outer fabric on to the worktable, right side facing down and press. Place the interlining over, matching seams and then lock stitch the length of all seams and half way across each width. Keep the fabrics flat and together throughout the whole making process.

3. Cut the interlining away on the sides and hem so that 4 cm (1½ in) of the main fabric is showing. Herringbone along the raw edge, taking care to pick up just one thread from the main fabric. Turn back the main fabric and herringbone stitch to the interlining on all three sides, mitring the corners as shown on page 8.

4. Place the inner curtain over, again lining up the seams. Pin to the under fabrics all around approximately 10 cm (4 in) from the edges. Score along the sides and hem of the curtain underneath and trim the inner curtain 2 cm (¾ in) outside these lines. Fold the fabric under and pin so that the two fabrics are exactly aligned.

5. Ladder stitch or slip stitch the sides and hems together using small stitches.

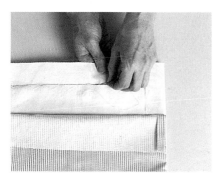

6. Measure from the bottom at 30 cm (12 in) intervals across the curtain, to mark your overall drop. Trim away the interlining along this line and herringbone to the outer curtain fabric. Trim away any excess fabric depending upon the heading you choose to make.

Canopies

Canopies need not be formal in the way that coronas and four poster beds are, and they need not be purely decorative. In many countries mosquito nets are an essential part of the bed drapes, and it is fun to incorporate them into more decorative bed hangings. You can either buy ready-made hoops with netting attached or make your own using metres (yards) of fine cotton or cotton and polyester netting. For safety, choose fabrics which are flame retardant.

For one island bedroom we stitched metres of fine cotton netting together to make a huge 'box' large enough to cover the bed completely. The centre and four corners had self ties stitched into the seams, then fitted to the ceiling with huge brass hooks. We untied four jute tasselled tiebacks and slipped them through the same corner hooks, to hold the netting out of the way during the day time.

For another bedroom, we made four single curtains which threaded on to a metal hoop fitted over the centre of the bed. The hoop was suspended on a chain which finished approximately 30 cm (12 in) below the ceiling. Four unlined bed curtains were knotted together above the hoop, draped back to each corner and tied. Each morning the net curtains are just twisted once around each of the bed curtains and dropped down at night to keep out unwanted bugs. These net curtains do need to be at least double fullness so that the sides meet and stay closed.

Summer canopies always look stunning with stripes from the narrowest ticking to the widest tent or sailing canvas. Choose fabrics which are washable and presentable, even if they crease. I always send unknown and stiff fabrics to the laundry, from where they return beautifully soft (make sure you ask them not to add starch) and with the shrinkage excess taken out.

One of the main principles of good design is that rooms should be changeable – so a bed canopy or curtains hanging for the winter months can transform easily to a fresher, brighter summer version. I like to choose sheer white linen curtains in the summer months which make way for heavily interlined weaves and prints in the winter.

Tropical prints in strong colour combinations also look wonderful for summer bed canopies, as do antique sheets, white or unbleached muslin, calico, freshly coloured chintzes, strong leafy prints and plain or printed Indian cotton panels and bedcovers. Hold curtains with tiebacks, cord loops, lengths of cord, canvas or leather strips, metal holdbacks or have small pillars or short bedposts made to drape the canopy curtains over.

A beautiful antique hand-quilted Welsh bedcover provided the inspiration for this summer bedroom. The pink and white striped bed curtains and padded bed head cover are made from mattress ticking.

DESIGN AND MAKE SOFT FURNISHINGS

Corona Curtains

Traditional draped corona curtains are quite complicated items, involving the back curtain being draped and upholstered to a frame fitted to the wall behind the bed. If you have an important bed and are using exquisite fabrics, or antique bed drapes which need alteration, you should ask for professional help from an upholsterer specialising in period pieces. The easiest way to tackle corona curtains is to make one large curtain incorporating the back and side curtains together.

You will need fabric for the outer side curtains, and for the inner curtains, so choose fabrics which complement each other and which are compatible for cleaning. Small prints, plain glazed cottons and fine stripes are suitable for the inner curtain, but the colours should be soft as this is the fabric you will see first on waking each morning. In many ways the inner curtain of the canopy will now become the most important fabric in the room, as your eye will immediately be drawn to the bed.

Choose from a long length of fabric to see how it looks as you enter the room. It should work well with the bedcover, and not overpower any other factor.

I personally dislike pink inner curtains because the canopy can resemble a large gaping mouth, yellow is not kind to skin colour first thing in the morning, a soft blue and cream stripe can look

grey, and a soft apricot, pretty when seen close to, can look rather sickly from a distance.

Edgings and trimmings, as always, are all important. The front edge will always look better with a binding, a narrow braid, fan edging braid or a fringe. Play with colours or use a tone which blends – not to stand out but to just add a finishing line. If your curtains are striped, pick up one

Bedcovers are the most versatile furnishings as they can be transformed into marvellous curtains.

of the colours in a plain cotton or cut fabric on the cross to bind.

Bindings, pipings and inset braids need to be made up with the curtains. Ribbons and inset borders will need to be stitched to the main fabric before making up.

MAKING UP

Measure and estimate fabric as shown on page 177. You will need to cut two outer curtains, which will fit from the centre of the corona to the back, inner curtains which will fit all around the corona and the lining for the inner curtain which will fit to the back of the corona as shown. The linings and inner curtains must be exactly the same widths.

1. Join the inner curtain widths, outer curtain widths and the lining. Press seams flat. If the front curtains are to be interlined, place one at a time on to the worktable and lock stitch the interlining in place.

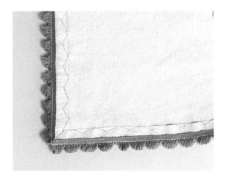

2. Stitch binding, piping or inset braid to the front sides and hem. Place one of the outer curtains on to the worktable and press flat. If no edging has been added at this stage, trim the interlining away 4 cm (1½ in) from the edge of the fabric and herringbone stitch in place. Press the 4 cm (1½ in) of fabric over and herringbone to the interlining. If piping or braid have been added, herringbone stitch the edging to hold it flat.

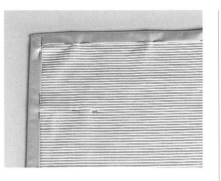

3. If the edge has been bound, press the edging outwards so that it can be brought around on to the inner curtain. Place the relevant outer edge of the inner curtain over, right side up and pin to the piece on the table. Lock stitch together on the seams and approximately 10 cm (4 in) from the outer edge. Fold the binding over, fold under and pin securely, making sure that the edging is even. Slip stitch to the main fabric with small stitches, and catching the interlining in at the same time to make a sure edge.

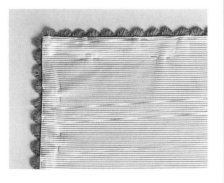

4. Otherwise, score along the edge of the curtain and trim away any excess fabric. Trim 2 cm (¾ in) outside this line. Fold under 2 cm (¾ in) and slip stitch to the edge of the outer curtain, piping or inset edging, using stitches of 5 mm–1 cm (¼–⅜ in) so that the stitches will not gape.

5. Continue to place the inner curtain over the lining, locking together along the seam lines. Finish the opposite outer curtain as the first. Pin the hems together but do not stitch. Level up the top if necessary and press 3 cm (1¼ in) to the front. Pin heading tape to the front and stitch along the top and bottom. Gather up and fit to the corona.

6. Drape the curtains back to either side. Mark the positions on the wall for the holdbacks or tiebacks, and fit. You will need to make a small hole in the curtain to thread on to the holdback, or to thread the tie back through. Snip carefully into the seam, and finish with buttonhole stitch all around once the hem has been finished. When you are happy that the back is falling straight and the canopy curtains are draped well, trim the back along the floor, allowing 3 cm (1¼ in) for turnings. Pin both fabrics together.

7. Fold both hem fabrics inside along the marked hemline and slip stitch together along the folded edges. Make sash ties or bows to hold back the canopy.

Half Tester Curtains

Follow the instructions for unlined, lined or interlined bed curtains, measuring the cuts as shown on pages 70, 72, and 73. If the half tester is made as a substantial frame, then the headings will be unseen from the front, so you can use bought heading tape to gather or pleat. If the frame is a metal or wooden pole, then the curtains will either hook into rings or tie around the poles with self ties, ribbon or fabric tabs, as the heading will be seen from both front and back. In this case, either hand gather, set heading tape between the inner and outer curtains, or stitch tape to the inside and make a fabric strip which will cover the tape when pulled up, and slip stitch top and bottom, holding the gathers with tiny stitches.

PELMETS

Make a template to design your pelmet shape and pin to the wood frame when you are satisfied with the size and shape. Cut the front and back fabrics and interlining. Allow two-and-a-half to three times fullness for both tester and corona pelmets and cut pieces for the outer and inner fabrics and interlining. Join, press seams and lock stitch together as for curtains. Treat the hem in the same way as the sides of the curtains, and bring the inner fabric right to the folded edge. Slip stitch and add your chosen trimming. If you are binding the edge, follow the curtain binding instructions.

The pelmet will fit to the front of the wooden board so make gathered or pinch pleated headings with the tape stitched on the inside. Stitch touch and close tape on to the pulled up heading and fit to the opposite side around the tester or corona.

Twist double ropes and stitch to cover the stitching lines.

SUN RAY PLEATING

Unless the half tester or corona is a wood or metal frame, the inside will need to be covered. The most attractive way is to pleat the fabric in a sun ray design.

1. Mark the centre of the corona at the front and back. Cut three fabric widths of fabric so that the length is 50 per cent longer than the widest angle of the corona.

2. Starting at the centre, place one piece of the fabric right side up, so that it overlaps the centre line by 2 cm (¾ in). Fold the fabric so that the first pleat is towards the middle line and aligns with the centre line.

3. Continue to fold the fabric, measuring the fold sizes carefully so that they are all equal on the outside edge. These pleats can be between 1.5 cm (⅝ in) and 3 cm (1¼ in) apart, based on personal preference and the amount of fabric available.

4. Keep the straight of grain correct, and pile the folds over each other on the inside edge. Only finger press the pleats, if the pleats are pressed too flat the finish will have no life or body. If the fabric gets too thick at the centre, cut away from underneath to trim the bulk, first making sure that each piece is secured at another point.

5. Staple underneath each pleat at the back, and staple each pleat on to the front of the corona around the shaping. The pleats will automatically form a semi-circle. Make a choux rosette or cover a large button to finish off the centre and cover the raw edges.

A favourite chintz in soft greens, greys and white, is lined with a tiny trefoil motif in aqua blue. The valance shows how well the two fabrics work together.

BEDCOVERS

As the bedcover is almost always the most dominant soft furnishing in the bedroom, it is well worth careful consideration. For this reason it is fun to make it in more than one fabric - sew together squares of complementary fabrics and border with braids, or experiment with patchworked pieces in a traditional design. The log cabin one used above is one of the simplest to follow and has the advantage that a very passable machine version can be made as long as you are careful to take consistent seam allowances. Or you can use several bedcovers together. Perhaps a plain cover with two plaid throws folded over; checks, plain colours and florals mixed in harmony; or tweeds and printed paisley with velvet. Fitted covers and duvets are two more alternatives.

Always try to use a large flat area to make bedcovers – it is important that the layers do not move against each other during the making process.

MAKING UP

1. Join the cut lengths of fabric together, always keeping a full width in the centre. Press the seams flat.

2. If you have chosen to shape the bottom corners, mark out the bed size on to the fabric, allowing 5 cm (2 in) each way for bedding underneath. Using a long ruler, measure from the bottom bed corners to the length decided, adding 3 cm (1¼ in) for the turnings. With the end of the ruler still on the bed corner, continue to measure at 3-4 cm (1¼-1½ in) intervals and mark with pins.

Join the pins up with a light pencil line and carefully cut around this curve.

3. If you are using interlining, cut the corners to match, place on to the wrong side of the fabric and lock stitch the seams together.

4. Fold the fabric over 3 cm (1¼ in) all around and herringbone stitch using stitches about 32 cm (12 in) in length. Place the lining over and lock stitch.

5. Score the lining along the edge of the bedcover and trim 1 cm (⅜ in) inside this line. Fold the lining under and slipstitch.

Four Posters and Footboards

The bedcovers for any bed which has legs or a footboard at the end will need to be cut or shaped to accommodate the obstruction. If at all possible, shape or cut below the mattress so that the cover will push down over the corner and hold the linen underneath in place. You will need to measure carefully and mark accurately on the bedcover the point at which any split will start and finish. It is sometimes easier to fit the made-up bedcover on to the bed with all bedding in place before taking the scissors to it.

Remember to add 2 cm (¾ in) for your seam allowance when cutting. Finish the cut out corner in the same manner as the bedcover sides and hem – shown here with a contrast bound edge. Or if the bedcover has a more decorative edging such as frills, scalloped shaping or a passementerie trim, simply self pipe around the two sides of the square. Slipstitch the lining in place with very small stitches as this corner will receive more pushing and pulling than the others.

Fitted Bedcovers

Fitted bedcovers should be lined throughout and may be interlined on the top. You may like to make decorative pillow covers, or to buy handworked linen covers for pillows which sit invitingly on top of the bedcover.

Or you may prefer to keep pillows hidden using decorative scatter cushions, in which case you will need to add a pillow gusset or attach a pillow flap.

Fitted bedcovers are difficult to use over unwieldy duvets, but work well over sheets and blankets which tuck neatly into the mattress.

MAKING UP

1. Join the cut lengths for the bedcover top as estimated and press the seams flat. Cut and join lining, and interlining, if used. Cut the skirt fabric and lining, join the seams and press. Leave to one side.

2. Lay the bedcover top on to the worktable, right side facing down. Place the interlining, if used, and then the lining over and lock stitch along the seam lines using 5 cm (2 in) stitches to hold the seams together securely. Press both fabrics together and pin around all edges at 10 cm (4 in) intervals. Trim away any excess lining and interlining so that all raw edges line up perfectly.

3. Pin the piping around, 2 cm (¾ in) from the raw edges and stitch close to the piping stitching.

4. Join the skirt lining to the main fabric. Place the skirt along the length of the worktable, wrong side facing down. Place the lining over, right side facing down and pin together along the hemline. Stitch 1.5–2 cm (⅝–¾ in) from the raw edges. If you are using a checked fabric then pin and stitch from the fabric side and follow the line of the checks.

The easiest way to handle a long piece like this, is to work along the length of the worktable, and then to fold the prepared fabric concertina-style, leaving this at the end of the table while you work on the next stage.

5. Press the skirt from the right side, pressing the lining away from the fabric. Turn over and fold the lining up so that 3 cm (1¼ in) of the main fabric is showing. Pin together along the top and trim away excess lining. Press under 2 cm (¾ in) of main fabric and lining at each open end and slipstitch along the fold to neaten.

6. Stitch a double gathering thread through, 1.5 cm and 2 cm (⅝ in and ¾ in) from the raw edges. Divide the length into 10 equal sections and mark each one with a coloured tack.

7. Divide the three sides of the bedcover top into 10 equal sections and mark with coloured tacks. Pin the skirt to the top, matching the relevant tacks. Pull up the gathering thread, one section at a time, and distribute the gathers evenly. Pin along the piping and across, so that the cross pins can be left in place to hold the gathers while stitching. You should have pins at approximately 2 cm (¾ in) intervals for the neatest finish.

8. Neaten the seam with binding. Cut a 10 cm (4 in) strip of main fabric, the width of the cover top. Stitch this strip along the top of the cover, right sides facing together, and as tight to the piping as possible. Press the strip under and in half to enclose the raw edges. Slipstitch to the lining, folding under the ends to neaten.

INTERLINED COVER

If you are using interlining, lock the interlining to the main fabric at step 2 and leave the lining to one side until the skirt has been attached. At step 6, lock stitch the lining to the interlining seams, press all the layers together and pin approximately 10 cm (4 in) from the outer edges, all around. Press the gathered seam and the cover top seam towards the cover top and herringbone to the interlining. Fold the lining under and slip stitch along the stitching line to enclose all raw edges.

PILLOWS

If you want to keep your pillows underneath this style of cover you will need to make some allowance for them. You will either need to add a pillow gusset or a pillow flap, the size of which will depend how many pillows you prefer.

Pillow gusset
Cut the fabric side pieces as shown in Measuring and Estimating (page 176). Stitch the gusset to the cover top and make up as before, following the instructions for the lined or the interlined cover, and cutting these pieces as needed.

Pillow flap
Cut out the fabric, lining and interlining pieces, join any seams and press flat. Place the fabric on to the worktable, right side down, and if interlining is used lock stitch to the seams. Trim in line with the top and 3 cm (1¼ in) in along the other three sides. Press the fabric 3 cm (1¼ in) to the wrong side along the hem and two sides and herringbone stitch to secure. Place the lining over and lock stitch to the seams. Trim away 1 cm (⅜ in) from each of the sides and hem, and slip stitch to cover the raw edges.

Leave on one side, and make up the cover following the instructions above. Attach to the bedcover at step 6.

DUVETS

Easy care cotton and polyester duvet covers have largely replaced crisp linen and cotton.

Designing and making your own covers will take no more time than choosing and buying ready-made ones and the finished result will be much more rewarding. Even if you have never stitched anything in your life before, they will not be beyond your reach.

Many fabrics may be used to make duvet covers – of course washability is essential, but you can prolong the life and the times between washing by always using a top sheet under the duvet.

One way to economise when the top fabric is rather expensive, is to use a sheet for the underside and your chosen fabric for the top only. Use washable country and floral prints with checks and stripes or put two similarly coloured but different scaled prints together. Re-vitalise traditional gingham and denim, use them on their own or with more sophisticated fabrics. Traditional French toile de jouy has long been a popular bedroom choice, and is especially lovely combined with simple Normandy striped cottons.

For variety, the top of the duvet cover could be lightly quilted, patchworked, or appliquéd with your own design. Co-ordinate your design with the headboard and valance coverings. Add interest to the design by mixing several colours, such as black, grey and red or French blue and white with a yellow ochre edging.

Decorative Details

How much smarter the most basic green checked fabric and white sheets have become below simply by using two scales of the same check. The large check forms a cheerful border on the duvet, while a narrow cornflower blue border has been added to the edge of the sheet for an effective contrast. Finish the duvet with fun teddy bear buttons, which make ideal fastenings for a child's, or grandchild's bedroom.

Self-fabric ties make a pretty edge for chintzes, stripes or toiles (right).

Buttonholes can be made by hand or with a machine setting: choose fun buttons like these teddies (below). Buttons can be substituted with toggles or leather balls if you use heavy workmanlike fabrics, such as denim, tweed and wool (right).

MAKING UP

Take the measurements for your duvet cover from an existing cover or add 2 cm (¾ in) each way to the actual duvet size. You can buy fabrics which are wide enough without seaming but the designs and colours are limited, so plan to join with French or flat seams which will not tear with constant washing. Add 10 cm (4 in) to the length to make plackets for the opening.

I prefer the fastenings to be at the bottom end but they can be put to one side, if you wish. Once you have chosen the style of fastening, add the relevant amount of fabric to your measurements.

No extra allowance will be needed for buttoned or tied fastenings. For straightforward fastenings (buttons or poppers) the top will fold under in three to make a strong edge for the top fastener or buttonhole and the bottom will fold in half to make a placket to hold the buttons or bottom fastener. For ties, the 10 cm (4 in) allowance will need to be cut away, the ties inserted and the raw edges folded under and slipstitched to enclose the seams. Added borders will need double the width of the finished border, plus seam allowances: button holes, eyelets or poppers will fix into the border.

Ties made in the same fabric as the cover provide an effective and practical fastening (left, centre). Instead of stitching the ties to the cover, use an eyelet kit and thread the ties through these for a really neat and stylish finish (left, bottom).

FOOT FLAP WITHOUT FASTENING

To keep a duvet in place, I often insert a foot flap – a strip of fabric set into the underside which can be tucked into the mattress to prevent feet escaping.

Make up a strip of fabric 50 cm (20 in) narrower than the duvet × 50 cm (20 in), turning the seams under on the bottom and sides. Allow 10 cm (4 in) extra length to the underside of the cover and cut across the width 35 cm (13¾ in) from the end. Stitch the flap to the main piece, right sides together and neaten the seam. Pin the 35 cm (13¾ in) piece back on, setting the flap seam 6 cm (2¾ in) down. Stitch together on either side of the flap. Fold the 8 cm (3¾ in) under twice and stitch across. Neaten the seams to the side of the flap.

Join the duvet top and bottom together around all four sides. Insert the duvet through the foot flap opening.

FOOT FLAP WITH FASTENING

If you want to add a flap but have designed a bottom fastening, make up the flap as before, allow only 4 cm (1½ in) extra to the length, cut away 27 cm (10¾ in) from the end and re-join to the main piece with the foot flap inserted between. Join the top and sides together and continue with your chosen fastening.

PILLOWS AND BOLSTERS

A bed is hardly dressed without its full complement of pillows – and often cushions – whether they are functional or purely decorative. The white pillow cover above is designed to be used as it is easily laundered; the more formal scalloped-edged Oxford cushion and the bordered scatter cushion are more for effect. Navy blue and white are always elegant and can be employed for the most formal bedrooms; plain colours and stripes are rewarding for the way in which they can be used together to different effect. Bolsters, originally used as pillows, are popular on day beds but are also making a comeback on standard beds – usually as decoration rather than as replacements for traditional pillows.

While there are many styles, patterns and colours of pillowcases available 'off the peg', you will pay a great deal for well-made, decorative pillowcases. And buying someone else's design is not nearly as much fun as designing and making your own.

The only time when I would not hesitate to buy pillowcases is when I am designing a bed which needs white linen. A pile of freshly starched, Oxford-style pillows with hand-stitched drawn thread edgings looks wonderful, clean and elegant. If you prefer a country look there are well made, beautifully hand-embroidered white cotton cases from Portugal, Madeira and the Far East, to mix with antique cushions, sheets and nightdress cases.

If you are in rather a hurry, you could buy the plainest white cases which you can then decorate without spending much time at all. Use rows of ribbons and braids: stitch along the sides or all around an Oxford edge or bind the edges with a plain contrast, polka dots and checks, tartans and plaids.

HOUSEWIFE STYLE

1. Measure the width and height of your pillow, add 1.5 cm (⅝ in) all around for seam allowances and an extra 8 cm (3¼ in) to the back width and 20 cm (8 in) to the front. It is usual to put the opening on the right hand side. Cut out two pieces.

2. Place the smaller piece on to the worktable, right side down. Turn the 8 cm (3¼ in) to the back. Fold under to make 4 cm (1⅝ in) and machine stitch along the fold line. Repeat with the front piece, using 5 cm (2 in) of the allowance.

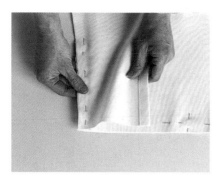

3. Place the front piece on to the table, right side facing up. Place the back piece over so that right sides are facing, and pin around three sides. Fold the flap over, pin to the other two sides along the top and bottom edges and stitch.

OXFORD STYLE

1. Measure the size of your pillow and add 2 cm (¾ in) seam allowances. Add the depth of the border – approximately 6 cm (2¼ in) – to each side. So a 70 × 50 cm (28 × 20 in) pillow will need to have a front piece 86 × 66 cm (34 × 26 in). The back will need to be cut as two pieces to make an opening for the pillow. Allow 14 cm (5½ in) extra to the opening side and 24 cm (9½ in) to the main back piece. (One piece 66 × 106 cm/26 × 41½ in and one piece 66 × 26 cm/ 26 × 10 in.) Cut out three pieces.

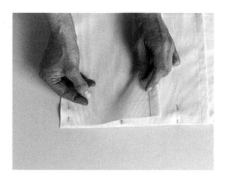

2. Make 2 cm (¾ in) double turnings along the opening edges of both back pieces. Place the pillow front on to the table, right side facing up. Place the main back piece over, matching up the three raw edges, and fold the opening edge back 20 cm (8 in). Place the smaller piece over, matching the raw edges, and overlapping the flap by 10 cm (4 in). Pin to secure. Stitch all around, neaten the seams and turn out. Press flat.

3. Measure a 6 cm (2¼ in) border inside the outer edge all around. Stitch along this line. Add narrow ribbon, braid or use a decorative stitch for individual detail.

Scalloped-edged Oxford

All Oxford-style pillow covers are made as above. For a scalloped edge, allow more depth for the border, and shape the edge using a template made by drawing around a wine glass or saucer. Make piping and stitch all around, following the shaped edge closely. Make up following the instructions above from step 2.

Frilled Pillow Covers

Any fabric can be frilled as long as the amount of fullness and the depth of frill are adjusted to suit each situation – a fine lawn will need three times fullness for body, but will flop if more than 8 cm (3¼ in) deep. In some cases a very floppy frill can be attractive; make a small template if you are at all unsure. Heavier fabrics such as velvet and damasks need less than double fullness and will be rather stiff if too short. Make up to between 8 cm (3¼ in) and 12 cm (4¾ in).

It is often the unexpected element that makes a design scheme work, and the lilac gingham is certainly a surprise with the subdued tones of a dog's tooth check bedcover and the rich browns and reds of the hand-printed cotton sheet and pillow cover.

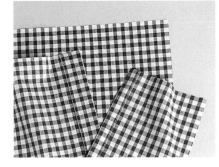

1. Measure your pillow and add 2 cm (¾ in) for seam allowances. Cut the front piece to these measurements. Add 8 cm (3¼ in) to the width and cut one back piece. Cut another piece the depth of the front piece and 14 cm (5½ in) wide. Use the 8 cm (3¼ in) piece to make a double turning on the opening side of the main back piece and 2 cm (¾ in) double turnings on the opening side of the smaller piece.

2. Cut widths of fabric to make the frill, allowing 4 cm (1½ in) for turnings and join with flat seams to make a loop. Make a 1 cm (⅜ in) double turning along the outside edge and stitch down, close to the fold line. Stitch a gathering thread 2 cm (¾ in) from the opposite raw edge. Divide the whole into 10 equal sections and mark with a coloured tacks.

3. Measure all around the pillow front and mark into 10 equal sections and mark with coloured tacks. Pipe around the edge. Pin the frill to the pillow front, matching the coloured tacks. Pull up the threads within each section and distribute the gathers evenly. Pin at approximately 2 cm (¾ in) intervals. Keep the raw edges lined up all the time so that the frill stays an even width.

4. Pin the larger back piece to the front, right sides together, along the three raw sides. Pin the smaller piece over, again matching the raw edges. Stitch all around, covering the frill stitching line. Neaten the seam, turn the pillowcase out and press.

FRILL FINISHES

Finish the frill with bound edges, stitching tape to the outer edges of the frill before gathering up.

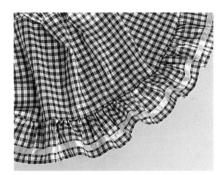

Ribbons or braids can be stitched parallel to the outer edge before gathering up.

Double frills need to be made from fabrics of the same content and structure to avoid any possible laundering problems.

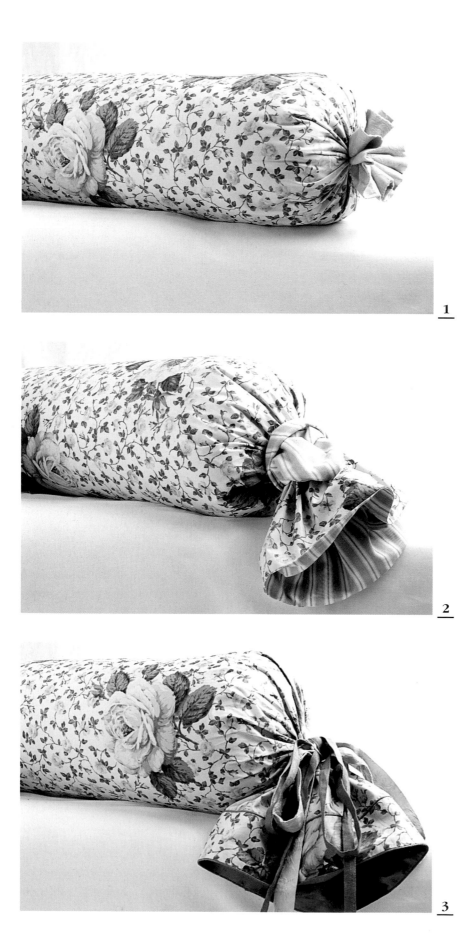

Bolsters

Bolsters are the cylindrical cushions which traditionally rested along the width of the bed and were used as we now use pillows. In particular, they are wonderful decorative and practical additions to day beds. Bolster fillings should always have a high proportion of down so that the bolster is light enough to handle easily, and soft enough to be really comfortable.

Bolster covers are very straightforward to make, at their simplest a cylinder needing one seam and two hems. These bolsters are made following the most basic method with six different tied ends.

Measure the circumference of the bolster and add 4 cm (1½ in) for the seam allowance. Measure the length of the bolster from halfway across each end and add 8 cm (3 in) for hems. These measurements form the basic fabric rectangle needed to cover the pad and any other finishes should be added to this measurement.

1. This 'flower' end was created with two strips of fabric in a contrast colour. Stitch the strips to either end, right sides together. Stitch a French seam along the length. Fold the end pieces in half, press the raw edges under and slip stitch to the seam line. Fill the bolster and tie the ends very tightly with ribbon or rouleau ties.
2. Here, the cover was made in two halves, adding 30 cm (12 in) to each end of the basic length.

DESIGN AND MAKE SOFT FURNISHINGS

Cut two pieces of main fabric and four pieces of contrast (yellow) fabric 35 (13½ in). Pin and stitch the four pieces of yellow to the four ends of the bolster pieces. Turn right sides out and join the two bolster pieces together with French seams. Neaten lining edges, fill the bolster and tie the ends.

3. This bolster cover is simply knotted and the end 'belled' out. Make the cover longer on each side than the basic pattern and line ends with a complementary fabric. Join the length with a flat fell or French seam. Neaten lining edges, fill the cover and tie ends into a loose knot.

4. Make the bolster cover 55 cm (22 in) longer each side than the basic pattern. Cut extra strips of main fabric to make a border at each end and contrast fabric for linings. Pipe around the two short ends of the bolster. Stitch the border strip to the same piping line. Pipe around this border. Stitch the lining piece to this stitching line. Using a flat fell seam, join the length of the bolster. Neaten lining edges, press and fold to the inside. Fill the cover and tie each end in a loose knot.

5. Picking up a secondary colour and using it for the piping adds an effective detail.

6. This cover is made 35 cm (14 in) longer at each end than the basic pattern. Join the length and hem in the usual way. Fill the bolster and tie with four rouleau ties made from a dark green fabric. Fan out the end to look like an open flower.

4

5

6

DRESSING TABLES

As purely feminine pieces of furniture, dressing tables can be embellished or simplified, but should reflect the character of the owner. Romantic layers of lace, organdie and muslin decorated with roses and ribbons; floral prints decorated with lace-edged frills; a plain chintz undercloth with an embroidered shawl draped over or silk tulle with rows of ribbons will be bliss for one person but anathema to another.

For practical purposes, the skirts are made up as curtains, to hang from a curtain track fitted beneath the tabletop. This means that they can open and close to access drawers or shelves and be removed easily for laundering.

If you are reclaiming an old table or desk, you may need to fit a new lid which extends 5-6 cm (2-2¾ in) in all directions to take the curtain track. Choose a narrow track which will bend tightly around the corners and hold the heading as straight as possible.

The lid may be upholstered with the valance stitched or tacked around, in which case a glass top should be cut to protect the fabric which cannot easily be cleaned. Alternatively, the lid and valance can be made as one, with the valance stitched to the top. To prevent the whole thing sliding around, small flaps need to be stitched inside – at each corner and halfway along each side should be adequate – and then pinned to the underside of the lid.

MAKING UP

Measure or make a template of the dressing table top. Measure the overall drop for the skirt and allow at least double fullness. Estimate the depth needed for the valance and check the proportions by pinning a strip of paper in position. Allow two or two-and-a-half times fullness for a gathered frill and three times fullness for box pleats.

Cut out the fabric pieces adding 1.5 cm (⅝ in) for all seams, 6 cm (2¼ in) for the skirt hems, 4 cm (1½ in) for the valance hem and 4 cm (1½ in) for the skirt heading. Cut out linings to match.

Fitting a dressing table into the corner provides a practical solution to an otherwise dead space. Meadow flowers on a ticking stripe line the delicate toile de jouy which gives such charming character to a country-style bedroom.

1. Pin the lining to the wrong side of the top piece. Tack together and make up as one. Make piping and pin all around. Snip as needed to accommodate corners and curves. Stitch close to the piping stitching line.

2. To make the valance, pin the fabric and lining together along the bottom long edge. Press the seam towards the lining and fold so that 2.5 cm (1 in) of main fabric shows on the back. Pin along the length and trim away excess lining. Stitch gathering threads 1.5 cm (⅝ in) from the raw edge or mark out the pleat positions allowing three times fabric for each finished pleat. If the dressing table is fitted into a recess, trim away any excess fabric at the ends and close the opening. If free standing, join the ends to make a complete circle.

3. Pin the valance to the top and stitch close to the stitching line. If the table fits into a corner and the valance does not extend to all sides, stitch small flaps to the other sides to enclose the raw edges. When the top is put back on to the dressing table, these flaps can be pinned to the underside to stop any slippage.

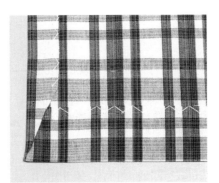

4. To make the skirt, join widths as necessary. Press a 6 cm (2¼ in) hem to the wrong side, press a side turning of 3 cm (1¼ in). Mitre the corners (see page 8) and herring-bone stitch all around.

5. Join lining widths as necessary. Place the lining over, wrong sides facing and lock stitch to the main fabric along the seams and halfway across each width. Score the lining around the hem and sides following the folded edge. Trim to this line. Fold the raw edges under 1.5 cm (⅝ in) at the sides and 3 cm (1¼ in) on the hem. Slip stitch neatly all around.

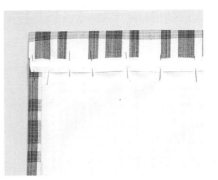

6. Measure the overall drop from the hem to the heading and fold the excess fabric over on to the lining. Pin and stitch curtain heading tape between 2 and 4 cm (¾-1¼ in) down – hook up a section and hang on to the track to test the drop and determine exactly how far down to stitch the tape.

7. Pull up the skirts and hook to the track, fit the top over the table and finger press the piping around the edge so that the valance falls straight. Pin flaps or tabs to the underside to prevent the top slipping around.

These curtains could be finished in many different ways. Try lining with a contrast colour, binding all around to pick up a colour or to contrast, or adding frills, fringes or braids to the hem to add weight and flounce.

STORAGE

Where to store things is a perennial problem: small items need to be kept together and yet separate from everything else. Covering boxes with paper or fabric is one solution. Or you can use fabric to cover clothes or for the bags shown above; designed to hold shoes, these are also suitable for items like scarves and tights.

To make this simple bag, fold a length of fabric in half with the right side inside and stitch along the two sides. Fold the open edge under twice to conceal the raw edge and stitch close to both fold lines. Leave a small opening near one seam to insert cord or tape which will be pulled up to close the opening. Or fit eyelets through all layers and thread through with thick cotton cord. If you want to make a contrast lining, make up two bags the same size and insert the inner into the outer before making the cord casing.

Clothes Covers

Long and short clothes bags hold suits, jackets and dresses in storage between seasons, or protect clothing while travelling. These really don't take long to make and once you have cut out the first one, all the others will be the same – just adjust the length as necessary. If you already own a suit cover, use it as a template to make your own; if not, base the top shaping around the size of a suit hanger and add approximately 7 cm (2¾ in) extra to the width at each side.

For a single item, the front and back of the bag could just be stitched together, but if you want to store several items in one bag, a gusset – cut to whatever depth you need – all around will allow the bag to expand. Similarly, the hole at the top can be cut large enough to take several hangers or small enough for one. The flap on the front of the cover shown here opens so that the clothes can be dropped inside – no dust can creep in – but a vertical front opening, buttoned or tied to close, would be a satisfactory alternative.

As with shoe bags, clothes bags need to be made from fabric which is easy to launder and press, in colours which will harmonize with your bedroom or dressing room. Washed denim chambray is a good universal choice as it can be masculine or feminine, and will team up well with strong checks or pretty floral prints.

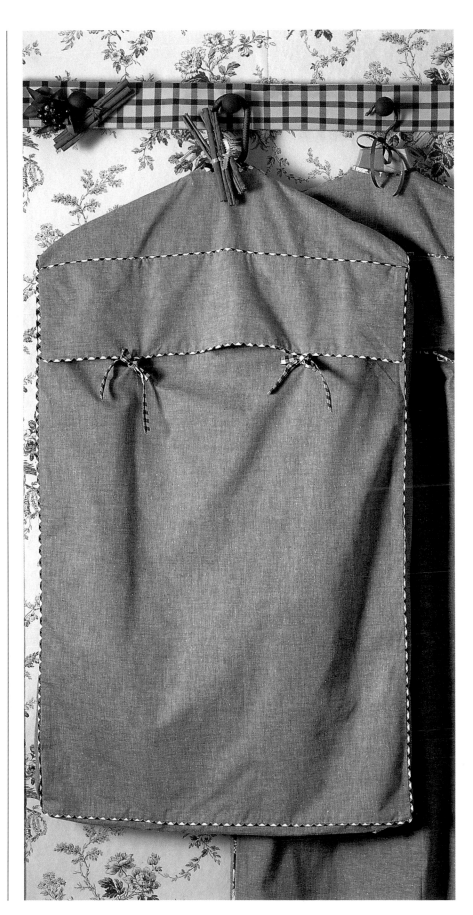

Shoe Boxes

Choose sturdy boxes and try to obtain ones of similar size so that they stack up neatly. Or open up one box and lid, and cut the same shapes from 2 mm (⅛ in) cardboard. Score the four sides of each and fold up, tape the ends together, so making a good solid box which can be copied easily. If you want to be able to see into the box without taking the lid off, cut a hole in one end and cover with clear acetate.

MAKING UP

You will need a 2.5 cm (1 in) brush, PVA glue and a suitable working surface.

The Lid

1. Cut a piece of fabric the length and width of the lid, twice the depth of the side, plus 1 cm (½ in). So a lid measuring 30 x 20 cm with a 2.5 cm side will need fabric 30 + 5 + 1 x 20 + 5 + 1, in other words 36 x 26 cm (12 x 8 x 1 in lid: 12 + 2 + ½ x 8 + 2 + ½ = 14½ x 10½ in). Paste a thin layer of glue all over the lid and place centrally on to the fabric. Smooth

thoroughly with the palm of your hand. Glue each long side and pull the fabric over the side of the lid, smoothing the fabric flat. Fold one short end over and pinch the sides together at one corner. Snip away excess fabric, 1 cm (½ in) from the corner. Repeat with the other corner on the same end.

2. Paste the short side of the lid and press down the flaps from the long sides. Paste lightly over these flaps, fold the other flaps under and press the whole side down. Repeat with the other end.

3. Paste inside the long sides of the lid and 1 cm (½ in) on to the inside of the lid. Press the long sides inside, pulling the fabric taut into the crease. Paste the short ends and press the fabric down. To line the lid, take the internal measurements and cut fabric to fit.

The box

4. Cut a piece of fabric the length and width of the box plus 2 cm (¾ in) and the depth of the box plus 3 cm (1¼ in). Paste the four sides with a thin, even layer of glue. Keep the fabric straight with equal overlaps at the top and bottom, starting 1 cm (½ in) on one short side. Follow on to the adjacent long side and then on to the remaining sides, keeping the fabric straight and smoothing out any air bubbles as you go. At the corner, cut the fabric to meet the edge and paste in place.

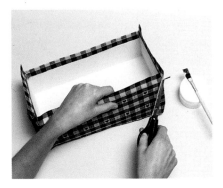

5. Snip down in to each corner and take a tiny nick out. The hole left should be approximately 2 mm (⅛ in) wide. Paste the inside of the box and press each side down in turn, pressing well into the corners and keeping the top edge even.

6. Take the same small strips of fabric from each bottom corner and press under one side at a time, cutting mitres at each end of the long sides to prevent a fabric lump at each corner. Cut a piece of lining for the base, 1 cm (½ in) smaller all round than the base measurements; paste in place.

If you wish to line the inside of the box, cut one piece of fabric to fit all around the four sides and deep enough to start 1 cm (½ in) from the top edge and to paste 1 cm (½ in) on to the inside base. Cut the base piece to fit exactly and paste all over the raw edges.

You might like to pad the top of the box, in which case cut a piece of polyester wadding to the exact size of the box lid and glue in place before covering with fabric. Don't paste the padding, just apply adhesive along the four sides.

Once you discover the satisfaction of making storage boxes you will probably be making and covering them over a period of years – so select fabrics which complement each other in colour and style that will easily mix and match.

AROUND THE HOME
CUSHIONS

Bright silks in varying tones and hues were made into basic scatter cushions for a quick, but effective, splash of colour on this formal striped sofa.

In the second half of this book, we look at various soft furnishings which are useful for almost any room in the house.

Individually styled cushions will add vital accents to a room scheme and will accessorise your chairs, sofas and beds. Scatter cushions, piped or unpiped, are the easiest to make and are a good starting point: a simple one in the right fabric and situation, with the corners square and the pattern well placed, is more effective than a mountain of complicated but poorly finished covers. They can be enhanced with frills and borders, buttons and stitching. Box cushions are more bulky and should either be small and decorative to place in front of a larger cushion or on a side chair or very large sofa. They can also be used for seats. Squab seat cushions are the answer for kitchen chairs.

Whatever type you decide on, choose your fabrics with care. A country-inspired interior will call for simplicity, rough textures, and practicality. Mixing fabrics – checks with florals and stripes, crunchy cottons and linens with wool tweeds – offers informality and practicality. A sophisticated town house will call for elegance, embellishment and detailed, but understated, design: silks, satins and sheers, the finest worked and woven linens and tonal mixes of similar fabrics.

Duck or goosedown makes the most luxurious and longest lasting filling, but is expensive. A high proportion of feather with some down provides a comfortable and affordable pad. Firm pads are now usually made from foam covered in a layer of polyester wadding or a quilted feather wrap.

BASIC CUSHIONS

Basic scatter cushions provide decoration and comfort, but need not be at all complicated to make. A simple basic cushion can add an instant splash of colour, and only takes minutes to make.

MAKING UP

Cut out two pieces of fabric, one for the front and one for the back, placing any pattern to its best advantage and allowing 1.5 cm (⅝ in) seam allowance all round.

1. Place the front and back pieces together, right sides facing. Snip or make notches through both layers, randomly on each side.

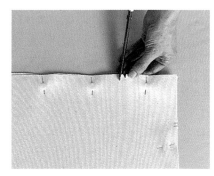

2. Pin the two pieces together along the bottom edge and stitch for 4 cm (1½ in) from each side. Put in the zip following instructions on page 11.

Although extremely simple to make, a group of scatter cushions can add a finishing flourish to any room. Instead of piped edges, these cushions have been trimmed with thick cord.

3. Open the zip about halfway and pin the other three cushion sides together, taking care to match the notches. Trim across each corner.

4. As far as possible, press the seams flat. Turn the cushion right side out and press the seam line along each side lightly.

Finishing Touches

● Stitch cord all around with small stitches, weaving into the cord and through the edge of the cushion cover so that stitches are invisible. Knot each corner and stitch in place.

● Inset fan edging braid by stitching it to the front piece before the zip is inserted.

● Cut and twisted fringes, tassels and braids can be stitched to two or four sides with small stitches holding each edge in place.

● Make a rolled edge by inserting a twist of polyester wadding or soft interlining against the outer edge once the cushion cover has been turned to the front. Stitch the roll in place using a decorative hand stitch. Alternatively, machine stitch and cover the line with cord.

DECORATIVE CUSHIONS

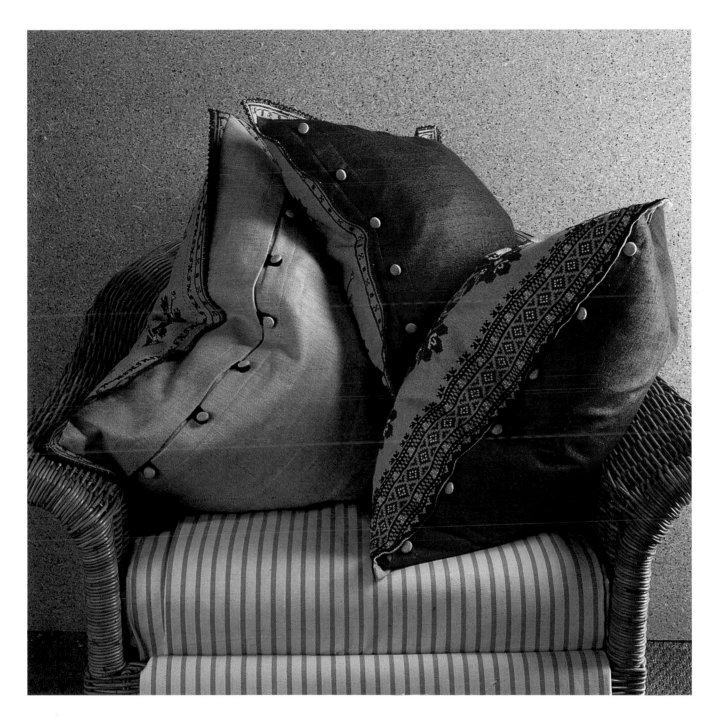

The cushions above are made from hand stitched panels from Bulgaria, backed with linen weave silks and finished with covered buttons and ribbon loops that echo the thread colours. Cushions decorated with piping, frills, buttons and borders are less dramatic – but equally effective.

Piped Cushions

Finish scatter cushions with contrasting or matching piping.

MAKING UP

1. Cut the cushion front and back, placing any pattern to its best advantage, and adding 1.5 cm (⅝ in) all round for seams. Cut a strip the width of the cushion × 7 cm (2¾ in) and match it to the bottom 7 cm (2¾ in) of the back piece. Make up piping to go all round.

2. Place the two pieces on to the worktable, right sides together and snip or notch randomly all around.

3. Press the bottom edge of the back piece under by 5 cm (2 in) and trim back to 2 cm (¾ in). Pin the extra strip along the fold line. Stitch together along the fold from each side, continuing along the fold lines.

4. Insert the zip following the instructions on page 10. Open the zip to roughly halfway.

5. Pin the piping to the front piece, starting from the bottom centre, snipping and folding hard into the corners. Pin and join following the instructions on page 9. Stitch on.

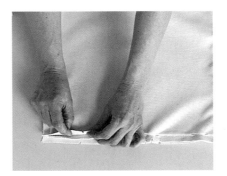

6. With right sides together, pin the front to the back, working from the front side, matching notches or snips. Sew inside the piping stitching line and very close to the piping cord.

7. Turn right side out. If any of the piping stitching is showing or the piping looks uneven, stitch around again. Trim the corners and stitch across them to secure. Finish the seams and turn out. Press gently along the piping lines and pull each corner square. Fill with the cushion pad, plumping it well to ensure that the corners have enough padding.

Decorative Options

1. Stitch decorative braids to your cushion front before adding the piping. Stitch two strips of 5 mm (¼ in) tape first and then two strips of 3 mm (⅛ in) tape over the top.

2. Scalloped borders in matching or contrasting fabric need to be made up and stitched to the piped cushion front before the front and back pieces are stitched together.

3. An easier way to make a scalloped border is to over-cut the cushion fronts and backs, cutting the shaped edge around the front piece only. Fine piping is a little difficult to add but need not be a problem if pinned carefully and snipped often so that it lies flat. Pin the front to the back and stitch from the front close to the piping. Snip away all excess fabric, turn out, press, pin and satin stitch together.

4. The cushion front can either be joined in three panels or can be made to appear as three sections by stitching the centre piece over the cushion front. Use braids or tapes to cover the joins, stitching close to each side. Pipe the cushion front and make up in the usual way.

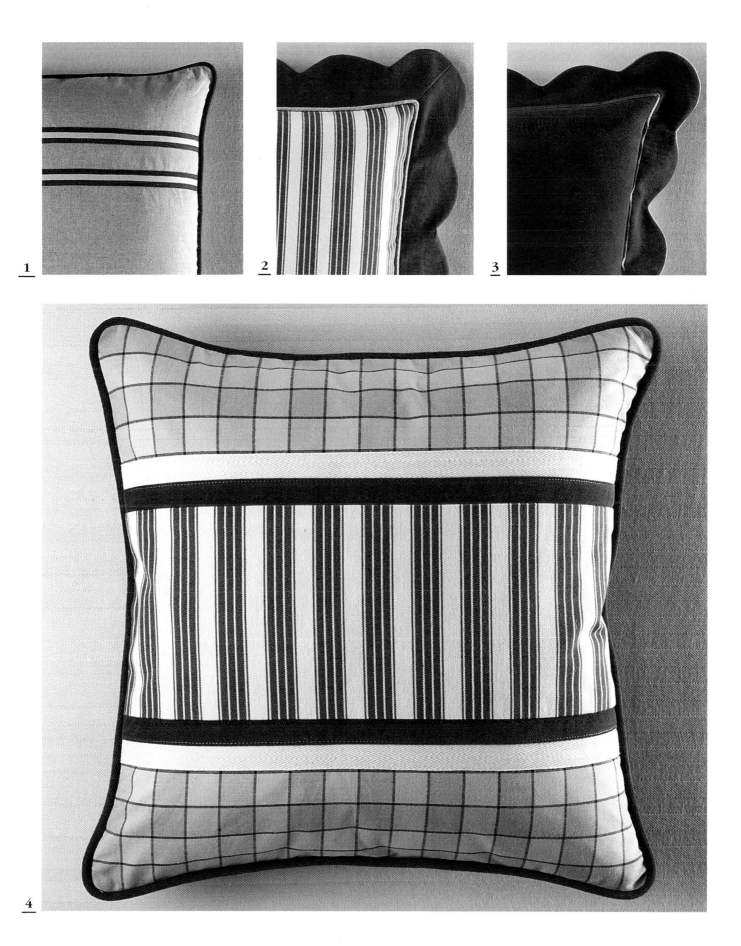

FRILLED CUSHIONS

Frilled edges are usually added to give a feminine touch, especially when used alongside floral fabrics, lace trimmings and bedroom furnishings. Frilled edges may be as a short, tight ruche or cut to be long and floppy, so adding weight to the sides which can improve the way a cushion sits on the arm of a chair or sofa, for instance.

Frills can be used with any fabric: do not feel restricted to florals.

MAKING UP

Cut pieces for the back and front, placing any pattern to its best advantage and adding 1.5 cm (⅝ in) all round for seams. Cut a strip of fabric the width of the cushion × 7 cm (2¾ in) and match to the bottom 7 cm (2¾ in) of the back. Make up piping to go all round. Cut strips for frills, allowing at least double fullness. For a simple frill allow twice the depth of the finished frill, plus seam allowance.

1. Press the bottom edge of the back piece under 5 cm (2 in) and trim to 2 cm (¾ in). Pin the extra strip to this piece, right sides together, along the fold line. Stitch together 4 cm (1½ in) from each side, along the fold line.

2. Insert the zip following the instructions on page 10. Open the zip to about halfway.

3. Pin piping to the front piece, starting at the centre bottom, snipping and folding firmly into each corner. Pin and join following the instructions on page 9.

4. Make up the frills, joining the strips together along the short sides. Press the seams flat, fold in half lengthways wrong sides together and stitch a gathering thread 1.3 cm (½ in) from the raw edges. Divide the frill length by eight and mark with coloured tacks. Also mark halfway along each side of the cushion front in the same way. Gather the frill slightly. Using the tacks as markers, pin the frill to the cushion front, matching the tacks to each corner and to each side.

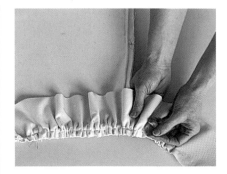

5. With the frill pinned at the coloured tacks, pull up the gathers evenly between these points. Pin along the piping line and across the piping. Stitch as close to the piping cord as possible, leaving the pins across the piping in place while stitching.

6. Remove the pins, turn the cushion over and check that the piping stitching line is not visible. If it is, re-stitch inside the previous line to ensure you have a really neat finish.

7. Pin the back of the cushion to the front, matching corners and notches. Stitch close to the piping line as before. Cut across the corners and stitch to secure. Turn right side out, pull corners square, press and fill with the pad.

I like to add frills to otherwise quite strong or 'masculine' fabrics, such as this strong navy and white stripe, rather than to make an overtly frilly cushion. The frill introduces a gentleness and softness to a formal situation.

OXFORD CUSHIONS

Fabric is folded under on the front and the back, along all four sides, and stitched to make flaps.

Add 25 cm (10 in) all round to the pad's dimensions. Cut the front piece to these and the back one to the same width but 4 cm (1½ in) longer.

1. Cut 20 cm (8 in) from the back piece. Pin the two pieces together, 2 cm (¾ in) from the raw edges. Stitch 16 cm (6¼ in) in from each side. Press. Insert the zip (page 10) and open it halfway.

Oxford cushions have borders which are folded under to produce two flaps all round (above), whereas a false Oxford cushion has the border made with just one stitching line. It is quite a formal finish, useful in contemporary schemes and with frilled and piped cushions to vary the style.

Linens and cottons in neutral shades have been a favourite for fashion and interior designers for quite some time. This impromptu slipcover (right) was put together in minutes when I found an antique sheet in the cupboard. The look was then completed with cushions in fine woven linens.

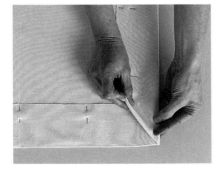

2. Place both pieces on the worktable, with the right sides facing down. Working with each piece consecutively, fold and press over 7 cm (2¾ in). Fold the corners under in turn, to make a false mitre. Pin in place.

3. Place the front piece on to the back piece, with wrong sides together. The corners should align so that each one is folded in the opposite way, and so that they lay flat. Pin all around, 5 cm (2 in) in from the outside edge.

4. Satin stitch all around following the pinned line. The flaps should be free, but firmly stitched, with no raw edges escaping. Open up the zip and fill with the cushion pad.

False Oxford

For this an inner line, which will contain the pad, is stitched on an unpiped cushion cover.

Add the border width to the pad width and allow 1.5 cm (⅝ in) all round for seams. Cut the front piece. Cut two back pieces to the same width but make one 12 cm (4¾ in) deeper and one 10 cm (2 in) shorter than the front piece.

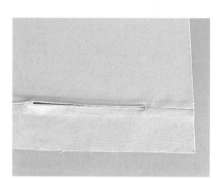

1. Press 2 cm (¾ in) under along the lower edge of the larger back piece. Pin the 12 cm (4¾ in) strip to it, along the field line and stitch 12 cm (4¾ in) in from either side. Insert the zip, as explained on page 10 and open halfway.

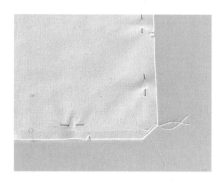

2. Pin the front and back pieces, right sides together. Stitch all round. Trim across the corners and sew over again to strengthen.

3. Neaten the seams and turn right side out. Press along all the sides and pin all around to prevent any slipping.

4. Measure the width of the border carefully from each side and mark a line with light pencil or vanishing pen. Pin across the line at approximately 4 cm (1½ in) intervals. Satin stitch closely along this line to define the border.

There are many ways to finish a border: try sewing several rows of satin stitch in the same colour or mixed colours to contrast or pick out the cushion fabric. Or stitch braid over the top with a straight stitching line. Satin stitch always takes more thread than you might expect, so make sure that the bobbin is full before each row.

A true Oxford cushion (above) – notice the two separate flaps – will sit comfortably into the back of almost any upholstered chair.

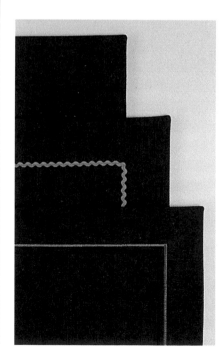

PIPED BORDERS

Separate borders can be piped onto the main cushion.

Cut the front piece to the pad size, allowing 1.5 cm (⅝ in) for seams. Cut the back one to the pad size plus the border width and seams. Allow 4 cm (1½ in) for the zip. Cut 11 cm (4¼ in) from the bottom. Stitch together again 12 cm (4¾ in) from each side and insert the zip (see page 10). Pipe the cushion front.

1. Cut four strips of fabric the width of the finished border plus 3 cm (1¼ in) for seams and the length of each side, plus two border widths. Pin one border strip to the bottom of the cushion front and one to the side, starting at the centre. Mark the first corner, unpin the strip and fold to make a right angle. Stitch together along this fold line.

2. Pin the border once again on to the cushion front, and join to the two corners. Mark carefully, repeating the folding and stitching instructions.

3. Repeat with the final corner. Stitch each side in turn, unpicking the stitching on each mitre 1.5 cm (⅝ in) so that the corner lies flat. Stitch as closely to the piping as possible, secure the stitching at each corner and start with the needle position exactly along the mitre line.

4. Stitch the back to the front, secure the corners and turn right sides out. Pin the front and back pieces together and stitch along the piping line through all layers.

If you enjoy whitework, cross stitching or any other stitchwork use your skills to embellish the bordered edges.

BUTTONS AND HAND STITCHING

Buttons as fastenings are infinitely more attractive (right) than present-day zippers. Machine-stitched buttonholes are perfectly satisfactory, but make hand sewn buttonholes for a really professional finish. If you are already *au fait* with hand stitching your buttonholes you will know how little effort is required for a very satisfying result. In any case, do take the plunge and make your fastening a feature on the front of the cushion.

Pintucks

Traditional dressmaking finishes and hand stitching are gradually being revived and re-introduced to soft furnishings by interior designers.

Pintucks are one of the most straightforward and adaptable of finishes. Fold tucks accurately and stitch with small machine or neat hand stitches.

Stitching pintucks together to form their own design is just one way to vary the traditional format. Keep main fabric, tucks and thread in tones of the same colour for a sophisticated look or match the thread to the main fabric with contrast tucks for a striking effect.

MAKING UP

Make a template of the cushion front in calico or scrap fabric, pinning rows of tucks in position as you wish, adjusting the amount and size until you are satisfied. Use the final template to cut the cushion front. Cut the back piece to the size of the pad plus 1.5 cm (⅝ in) seam allowance.

1. If the pintucks are to be in a contrasting fabric, cut the main fabric into strips and stitch sections in to correspond with the number and width of tucks. Press along the centre of the first tuck and pin fabrics together at right angles to the tuck. Using the machine foot guide for accuracy, stitch along the length of the tuck, parallel to the folded line. Repeat with the other tucks. Press and make up the cushion cover following the instructions on page 18.

2. For self-fabric tucks, plan the stitched design on the template and mark each tuck accordingly with a fine pencil or marking tacks. Hand stitch tucks together with embroidery thread. Press and make up the cushion cover following the instructions on page 100.

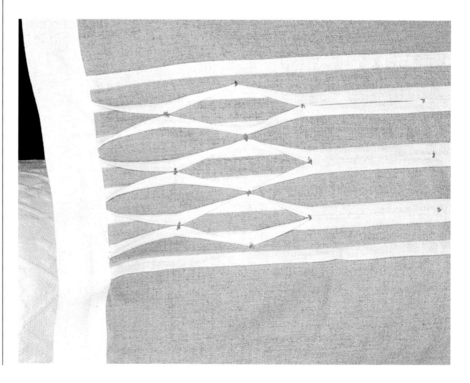

Purely decorative, pintucks can be as subtle as you wish: tiny tucks in neat rows giving a delicate air to fine cotton or linen; or deliberately striking: deeper tucks across the whole cushion, each in a different colour.

Rouleau loops and tiny fabric covered buttons do not just belong on wedding dresses and couture gowns. Fine woven fabrics make the best loops – use cotton, silk or linen.

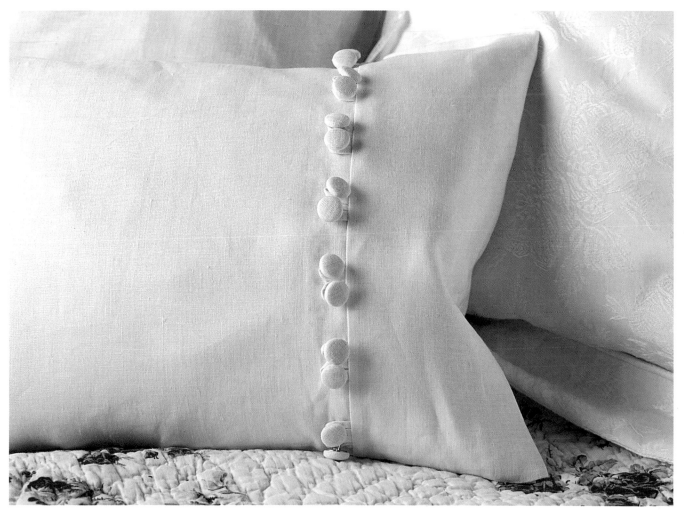

BOX CUSHIONS

1. These are ideal for seats. Cut out the pieces and make the piping as on page 9.

2. Place the top and bottom pieces flat on to the worktable, exactly together. Snip irregular marks on all four sides using single, double and triple cuts at 10–20 cm (4–8 in) intervals.

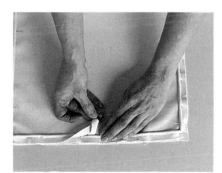

3. Starting on the back edge, pin piping to the right side of the fabric, all round the top and bottom pieces. Pin so that the stitching line will be on the seam allowance. At the corners, snip right up to the stitching line on the piping, open out the cut so that the piping forms a tight corner. Pin securely. Join the piping as instructed on page 9.

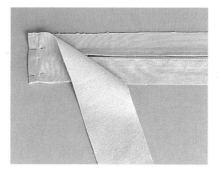

4. Stitch on piping. Insert the zip into the gusset strip following the instructions on page 10. Join to the other gusset piece.

5. Starting with the free end of the gusset, pin one side of the gusset to the top of the cover. Match the seam allowance and pin on to the piping line. Cut into the corners, right up to the seam allowance to give a good square corner.

6. Where the zip gusset and the main gusset meet, pin together and stitch the short seam before finishing the pinning. Cut away any excess fabric. Stitch all round as close to the piping as possible. Check from the front that the first piping stitching line is not visible. If it is, stitch around again from the other side, making sure that your stitching line is inside the first one.

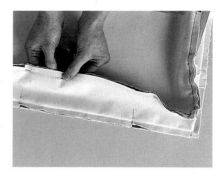

7. Pin the other side of the cover to the opposite side of the gusset. Start at the back and, matching the seam allowances, pin along the piping line. Match up the notched marks by scoring a pin line from a notch on the stitched side, across the gusset, following the fabric grain. At each corner score a pin line from the stitched corner to the opposite side of the gusset to align the corners exactly. Snip into the seam allowance. This cut should form the corner. Stitch all around.

8. Cut across the corners to within 5 mm (¼ in) of the stitching. Neaten the seam, open up the zip and turn the cover to the right side. Push each corner to a good shape with a point turner or the end of the scissors. Press all over. Lightly press the seam allowances away from the gusset. Fill the cover with the pad, checking that the filling fits right into each corner.

> A box cushion has a gusset between the top and bottom pieces, so should really be described as a 'boxed cushion'.

Round Box Cushions

These are made in the same way as any other box cushion, but as the fastening into the gusset is likely to be all too visible, it is usually inserted right across the back.

Take extra care pinning the piping around the circles, snipping the gusset at 1 cm (⅜ in) intervals to prevent the fabric puckering.

The fastening across the back might be a zip or you can experiment with other options, such as buttons with buttonholes or loops.

Make the back in two sections. Cut two half circles and add 4 cm (1½ in) to the width of one and 7 cm (2¾ in) to the other. Make a double turning of 2 cm (¾ in) on both pieces. Place one over the other to form a complete circle and stitch across the join.

Stitch on buttons and buttonholes or tape loops.

I made these cushions to hide an unattractive guest bedroom chair using offcuts from the curtains, the bedcover and the scatter cushions adding just a few other floral chintzes from other rooms. Genuine hand stitched patchwork is a treat to see and to do, but it is not always possible to give the necessary time, so these cut squares were quickly machine stitched, first into lengths and then the lengths into two squares, and made up into box cushions with plain gussets and backs.

Shaped Box Cushions

Box cushions for any seat shape are made following the same instructions. See page 182 for measuring and making a template. Wicker chairs are shaped around the back.

Box cushions need to be shaped to fit snugly around the arm of a sofa or armchair, into a shaped seat, or on to a shaped stool.

Wicker and garden chairs almost always have seats which are straight along the front and then shaped at the back. Shaped cushions may be turned over so that top and bottom wear equally, but can never be turned back to front, so fastenings must be made into the centre of the gusset. Extend the opening as far around the shaping as is necessary for the pad to be removed easily. On seat cushions, this will be around the length of the curve. Sofa back cushions will be shaped on one side only and chair cushions on both sides, as they fit around the arms. Open approximately 10 cm (4 in) along a straight side and as far around the arm side as possible without being visible. Never try to make small openings on large covers as heavy pads are very difficult to squeeze in.

SQUAB SEAT CUSHIONS

Kitchen chairs are made to be easily moveable and practical to clean, are often wooden or wooden with rush or caned seats but can rarely be described as comfortable. Metal chairs although decorative, are only designed for short term comfort. However, piped squab cushions make even an uncomfortable seat pleasing to sit on. Buttoning can added an extra decorative accent.

MAKING UP

Make a template of the chair seat and buy or make a cushion pad as described on page 186.

1. Cut two pieces for the top and bottom allowing the depth of the seat pad and 2 cm (¾ in) seam allowance all around, place together and cut balance marks on each side to help re-matching later.

2. Make up enough piping to go around the squab, (or use flanged cord). Pin the piping all round the bottom piece on the right side of the fabric. The piping stitching line should be on the seam allowance, raw edges matching. Snip at regular intervals to keep the piping flat, fold tight into the corners and join, following the instructions on page 9.

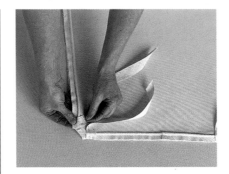

3. Make up ties and pin to the piping line, positioned to either side of the chair legs. Stitch to the seam several times. These ties will take a lot of strain, so strengthening them now could save a lot of irritation and fiddly repairs later.

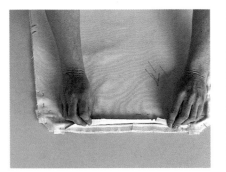

4. Pin the front and back piece right sides together between the back legs. Stitch for 2–3 cm (¾–1¼ in) from either side, close to the piping. Insert the zip, following the instructions on page 10. Open up the zip and pin around the other three sides. Match notches exactly. Stitch close to the piping, inside the piping stitching line.

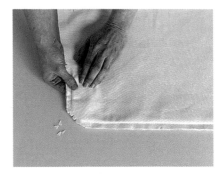

5. Snip into the corners, turn to the right side and check that the piping is stitched tightly and evenly. If not, stitch around again, pushing the machine foot close to the piping cord. Neaten the seam and turn right sides out.

Shaping

Some squab seats have quite complicated shaping around either the back or the front legs. Cut the fabric to your template and snip and bend piping so that it lies flat. You might prefer to choose a finer but tightly woven fabric for the piping so that it is easier to handle.

Use feather filled pads for a soft, informal look or foam or hair pads for a more solid looking seat. For a country kitchen or bedroom chair, add a frilled or straight skirt at the end of step 2, finishing at either side of the legs.

An elegant piped squab seat cushion with sash ties was quite straight-forward to make and adds comfort and discreet decoration to this rather formal metal chair.

BUTTONING

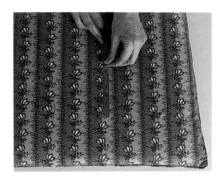

1. Either mark the template with the button positions or place buttons on to the pad and pin in place. Measure the distances between each button point and mark with a soft pencil or vanishing pen. These marks will be covered by the buttons. If you are as yet unsure of the position, use crossed pins. Mark exactly the same positions on the bottom piece.

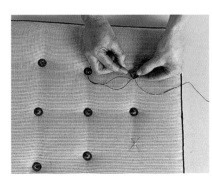

2. Using heavy duty thread and a strong needle, push through from the underside to the top. Thread through a button and knot. Push the needle back through to within 4 mm (¼ in) of the first hole. Thread through the button or straight into the underside, and pull the threads tightly to give a slight indentation in the pad. Knot three times and cut the threads.

Cleaning

If the squab is for occasional use and unlikely to be cleaned often, omit the zip and slip stitch the opening closed by hand.

To clean the squab, cut the threads, remove the cover and launder according to the type of fabric used. Replace the cover and re-stitch when clean and dry.

Contrast piping and buttoning make a boxed squab very striking and suitable for the most formal of rooms. Period dining chairs often have caned seats which need squab cushions for comfort. Traditional damasks and brocades or simple woven stripes all benefit from piping and buttoning.

CHAIR LEG TIES

Squab cushions need to be securely fixed to the back legs of your chair. Ties should be stitched very firmly to the seam inside and long enough to tie or button tightly without allowing too much movement.

Box squab cushions are deeper than piped squabs so are suitable for dining chairs and can give some height to chairs which are slightly too low for comfort.

Make the seat template and pad as before, fit the zip between the back chair legs and stitch ties between the gusset, but make up following the instructions for box cushions on page 113.

1. Knotted ribbon ends hold a single bead in place. Gilded or pearl drops, multicoloured or wooden beads would make equally effective decorations used singly or in long rows.
2. Stitch buttons and make buttonholes into petersham ribbon or self ties for a smart finish.
3. Petersham or double-sided satin ribbon is tied in decorative bows which also holds the pad to the chair seat. Use gingham ribbon or woven Tyrolean braid for children's and kitchen chair seats.
4. Make rouleau or folded ties from the main cushion or piping fabric or use ribbon, cotton or petersham which performs the same function. Strap around the chair leg to hold the pad in place and decorate the leg at the same time.

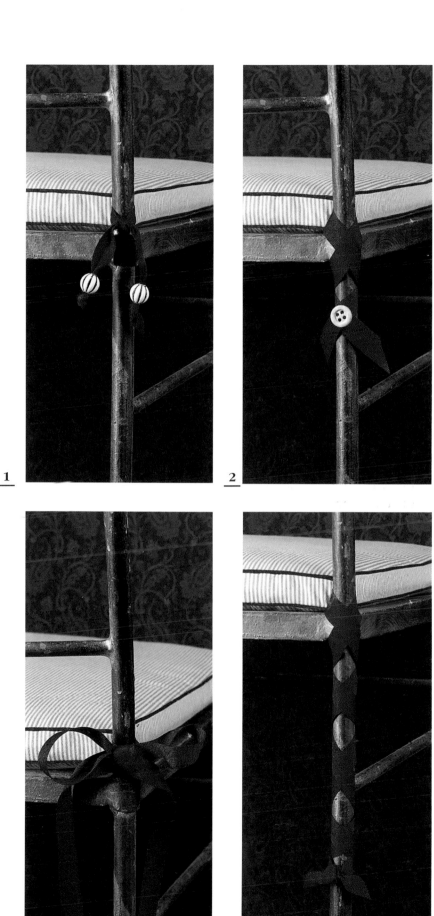

BLINDS

A simple mattress ticking is used in a formal colour combination and the folds are buttoned with dark green chintz-covered tailors' buttons. London blinds like this one are made in the same manner as Austrian blinds but the fullness is incorporated in pleats. Follow the instructions and directions on page 129.

Blinds are both decorative and a sensible window treatment. Because they are made of fabric they help to deaden noise and provide insulation from the cold outside; and they also add a dimension of cosiness, colour and texture. They can be made to fit different shapes and uses, and will still be raised and lowered efficiently with the minimum of fuss. Combined with long curtains where a radiator or other obstruction prevents full-length drawing curtains, they become the functioning unit while the curtaining provides style, atmosphere and balance. And they are especially useful in rooms where water is in constant use: above a kitchen sink, near a shower or bath, in a butler's pantry or utility room.

In style they vary from roller blinds – the most basic type – to elaborately flounced festoons. Rolled up blinds are the answer for children's bedrooms, cloakrooms, conservatories and any small windows that are awkward to dress, while a Roman blind is ideal above a kitchen sink as it will cover the window without adding clutter and can easily be pulled away from sills, taps and utensils. Austrian blinds are a rather more subdued version of festoons – they were originally called by this name – and lend themselves to a variety of different headings.

All in all, blinds can be as simple or as complicated as you wish; they can be plain and functional, decorative and functional – or just decorative. Whatever you decide, they will be a supremely practical option.

DESIGN AND MAKE SOFT FURNISHINGS

ROLLER BLINDS

Roller blinds can be made at home using your own fabric to match or tone with your other soft furnishings. You will need first to purchase a roller blind kit, available from specialist curtain fittings suppliers or large department stores. This kit will contain the rod and window fixings, the bottom batten, cord and a cord holder. You will need to make your fabric rigid enough to hang straight in the window yet flexible enough to be able to roll up neatly. A special stiffening spray or paste will be available from the same suppliers. Sometimes you can buy specially stiffened fabrics or Holland linen which are ideal if you just want to use the blind to protect furnishings from the sunlight; but if the blind is to be a feature in its own right, then you will probably want to use your own choice of colour and design.

The main advantage with a roller blind is that the roller can easily be fitted behind a pelmet, another blind, or a fixed curtain heading, to pull up completely out of sight. (A good example, for those wanting a purely functional blind which can be totally hidden, appears on page 179). If you only have a very small window in the house and wish to retain as much light as possible, roller blinds will fit right into the recess, against the window and will pull up into the depth of the top window frame.

Usually the roller blind is fitted so that the roller is in front of the blind when it is down. You can, however, change this. If the spring mechanism is reverse rolled, the roll will be behind the blind and therefore invisible.

I often make a small covered 'pelmet' board in the same fabric and fit it in front of the top of the blind so that the 'mechanics' are completely hidden. Just cover a 10 cm (4 in) deep piece of wood or MDF board with the chosen fabric, fix small brackets to the back, and screw into the ceiling in front of the blind.

MAKING UP

1. You must cut the fabric so that it fits between the fittings. This will be narrower than the measured width, so cut the roller to size first. Finish the edge with a straight or zigzag stitch to prevent the edges fraying.

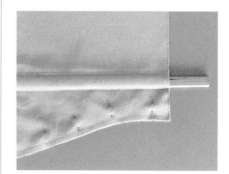

2. Shape the lower edge as you wish. Make a facing and attach it to the back of the hem. Stitch a pocket for the rod and stitch together at the lower edge to strengthen. Test the batten for fit.

3. Take the fabric outside and spray or paste with the stiffening solution. Leave to dry.

4. On the worktable, press the fabric. Check with your set square and with the sides and end of the table, that the top of the blind is absolutely square. Remove the sticky tape from the roller bar and carefully position the top of the blind along the marked line. Be careful not to stretch the fabric at all. Fix in position with small upholstery gimp pins.

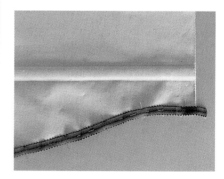

5. Add any trimming to the lower edge and glue in place. Hold with cross pins until the glue dries.

An attractive patterned roller blind with a gently scalloped edge serves to keep out the morning light, allowing the soft muslin to filter the sunlight during the day.

ROLLED UP BLINDS

Rolled up blinds can be fitted inside or outside the window recess and be made as full or as flat as you wish. They may be lined or unlined, and can easily be completely hand-sewn. They operate with tapes which tie at the bottom of the blind at whichever level you choose to leave it. Experiment with different edgings, borders, patterns and lining colours. The ones above are made from inexpensive artists' linen and bound with curtain heading tape. Cascade blinds are very similar to make but have rings and cords to operate them.

MAKING UP

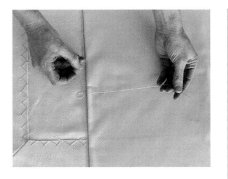

1. Add 25 cm (10 in) to the width of the fitting and cut the fabric and lining following the instructions on page 17. Place the fabric on to the worktable, wrong side facing up. Press the sides over by 12 cm (4¾ in) and the hem by the same amount. Mitre the corners following the instructions on page 8. Herringbone the raw edges along both sides and hem, ladder stitching the mitre.

This duck print blind is neatly raised and lowered with these threaded cords: a simple but very effective device.

2. Place the lining over the top fabric, matching the seams. Lock stitch the lining to the main fabric on each seam and three times across each width.

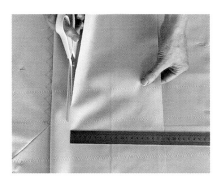

3. Using the scissors, score the lining along the folded edges of the blind. Trim the excess lining 8 cm (3¼ in) away from this line.

4. Fold the edges of the lining under by 2 cm (¾ in) to leave 10 cm (4 in) of main fabric showing on the sides and hem. Neatly slip stitch in place.

5. Carefully measure up from the hem at 30 cm (12 in) intervals to mark the overall drop. Pin in a line along the overall drop and then make the heading.

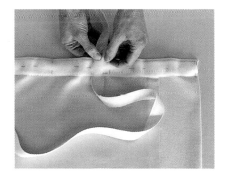

6. The usual fitting for flat blinds is touch and close tape. Trim the fabric to 1.5 cm (⅝ in) above the overall drop line, fold over and press. Pin on the touch and close tape and machine in place. Stitch ties, tapes or ribbons in place.

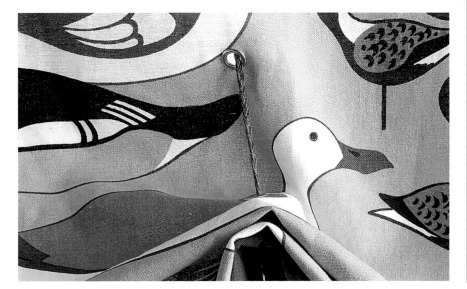

DESIGN AND MAKE SOFT FURNISHINGS

1

2

3

Hooks and Ties

1. A row of wrought iron pigs make amusing hooks to hold this kitchen blind in place. Checked fabrics always look just that bit smarter finished with a binding, whether plain or in self-fabric cut on the cross.

For a 3 cm (1¼ in) border, cut strips on the cross 12 cm (4¾ in) wide. Stitch together to make one length which will fit all around the blind and follow the instructions for binding edges on page 9. Stitch 3 cm (1¼ in) from the raw edges and take care to keep the checks lined up, whether on the straight or on the cross.

Make ties from cross-cut fabric, following the instructions on page

8. Take care not to stretch the bias edge; always press straight down rather than pushing the iron along the fabric, and use the largest machine stitch.

This blind can be made easily into a curtain by using the same ties to catch the fabric back to one side. This method of fitting is ideal if a window covering is needed only occasionally, perhaps in a guest bedroom.

2. Thirty per cent extra fabric was added to the blind fitting width to produce the swagged hemline. The extra fullness has been contained at the heading in four inverted pleats. Lining the chintz with a striped fabric, picking up the same red and green tones, gives an interesting finish when the blind is rolled up.

3. Checks and stripes have been used together ever since fabric was first woven and they still always look good combined within one room or one window treatment. The size, colour and balance of scale allow stripes and checks to look either very sophisticated or traditionally country in style.

The attached pelmet heading was lined and made up in the same way as the blind and stitched along the top with the front of the heading against the lining of the blind, folded to the front and pressed. Eyelet holes were cut at equal intervals across the top of the blind and eyelets fitted following the manufacturer's instructions supplied with the kit.

CASCADE BLINDS

1. Place fabric on to the work-table, right side facing down. Fold over the sides by 10–20 cm (4–8 in) depending on how much drop you want to see at each side; fold up the hem by 12 cm (4¾ in). Mitre the corners following instructions on page 8. Cut away the excess fabric inside the corners by first trimming off the triangle of fabric, as shown.

2. Cut away the remaining excess fabric, as shown, to give a neat finish. Hold the corners up to the light to make sure that there are only parallel lines of fabric showing through.

Left: Cotton duck was laundered first to soften the fabric. Blue and white striped piping adds some shape and just a touch of detail.

3. Herringbone stitch all the raw edges and ladder stitch along the mitred corner. Place lining over, matching seams. Fold back along the herringboned edges and trim 4 cm (2½ in) from the fold.

4. Fold lining under by 2 cm (¾ in) and pin down.

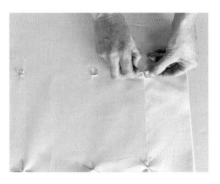

5. Mark the ring positions with crossed pins, measuring carefully between each one. Stitch each ring securely in place.

Rows of rings are stitched to the back and strings or cords threaded through these operate the blind. The number of rows governs the number and width of the swags; the vertical distance between the rings determines the size of the pleats and folds.

6. Measure at 30 cm (12 in) intervals from the hemline to the top to mark the overall drop line. Fold over along this line and trim the excess fabric to 1.5 cm (⅝ in) from the folded line. Pin touch and close tape in position and stitch in place along both sides.

7. Thread the cords from the bottom to the top of the blind, making sure they are long enough to return to the cord holder. Stitch the ends of the cords together to prevent the knots coming undone. Cut a wooden or metal rod, cover with lining and stitch in line with the bottom ring position along the top of the hemline. This will hold the blind straight at the bottom.

Formal Cascades

More formal cascade blinds (below) can be made if there is no fullness added to the width and the rows of rings and cords to pull up the blind are stitched closely enough together to prevent the fabric dipping in between. The edges are piped to stiffen them and the bottom edge is held straight with a covered wooden or metal rod.

A shortened rod allows the sides to pleat in smaller gathers as the blind is raised and lowered. This adds interest with detracting from the uncluttered lines. Five rows of rings and cords set at 20 cm (8 in) intervals operate the blind and control the form.

MAKING A PIPED EDGE

1. Cut away the amount allowed for the sides, facing or turnings. Make up enough piping, pin and stitch to the front of the blind. Stitch the borders and hem back to the blind, leaving the corners open.

2. Press the facings back, pin and cut across the corners to mitre.

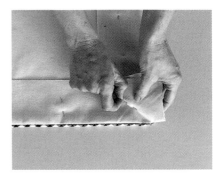

3. Slipstitch across the mitre and herringbone the raw edges.

ROMAN BLINDS

Roman blinds are a neat and smart answer to difficult windows like this kitchen one where there is no room for curtains to stack back – and they need less than half the fabric required for curtains. A Roman blind should never be more than 220 cm (86 in) wide. The rods will start to bend and the blind will not pull up evenly beyond this width. It is important to choose good quality, firm fabric for a wide blind, and one which will not pucker when sewn. Measure the blind very accurately and make it carefully to prevent either ugly gaps or fabrics rubbing together.

MAKING UP

1. Press the sides of the lining 3 cm (1¼ in) to the wrong side and pin in place. Cut the hemline of the lining straight, using either the set square or two sides of the worktable for accuracy.

2. Using a soft pencil or vanishing marker, measure up from the hemline and mark the stitching lines for the rod pockets. Pin the folds and stitch in place, keeping the sides even and stitching from one direction to prevent the fabric pulling.

3. Place the main fabric right side facing down on to the worktable, flatten it out with a metre rule or yardstick and turn in the sides by 6 cm (2¼ in). Turn up the 6 cm (2¼ in) hem allowance and fold the bottom corner over to mitre.

4. Leave open, but herringbone the sides and hem.

5. If the blind is to be interlined, place the interlining on top of the main fabric before turning in the sides. Fold the sides over and press. Unfold and trim the interlining back to the folded lines. Herringbone the interlining to the fold lines. Continue to follow the instructions, making up the main fabric and interlining as one.

6. Place the lining over the main fabric, pockets outwards. Carefully line up seams and hemline. Pin the sides securely. Pin each of the pocket stitching lines to the blind with pins at right angles to the stitching and with the pockets facing upwards. Slip stitch the sides between the pockets.

7. Machine stitch along the pocket lines, stitching from one direction to avoid the fabric pulling to one side. Measure from the hem upwards at 30 cm (12 in) intervals across the blind to mark the finished length. Trim the excess fabric to 2 cm (¾ in) from the finished length, fold over and pin a strip of touch and close tape to cover the raw edge. Stitch along the top and bottom of the strip.

8. With the blind face down on the table again, insert one rod into each pocket and the lath into the bottom pocket. Stitch the ends of the pockets to close. (When the blind is cleaned the rods can easily slide out of the pockets and be replaced later.)

9. Mark the ring positions, starting at 5 cm (2 in) in from each side and allowing three to four rows per width. Stitch the rings securely in position to the top of the rod pockets.

10. Thread the cords from the bottom to the top of the blind, making sure they are long enough to return to the cord holder. Stitch the ends of the cords together to prevent the knots coming undone.

Small recessed windows are difficult to dress in a traditional way with curtains, as curtaining fitted outside rather overpowers the size of the window, while inside it takes most of the light. Roman blinds are the perfect solution, and can be used to dress the window in a subtle way, without interfering with either the shape or the incoming light.

BINDING EDGES

A useful size for edging is 1.5 cm (⅝ in). This can be adjusted a little either way, slightly less for a fine fabric or a narrow blind and slightly more for a heavy fabric and a wider blind. Order your binding fabrics to be at least the length of the blind so that there are as few joins as possible.

EDGING A LINED OR UNLINED BLIND

1. Cut and join enough strips of 6 cm (2¼ in) wide fabric to bind all the way around. Join strips on the cross to reduce the bulk when the fabric is folded over.

2. Place the blind fabric flat on the worktable, with the right side facing up. Pin the edging strip along one long side as shown. Stop pinning 1.5 cm (⅝ in) from the corner. Fold the edging over at a right angle and continue pinning along the hemline. Repeat with the other corner and side.

3. Stitch all around, at 1.4 cm (just under ⅝ in) from the raw edges. Stop stitching 1.4 cm (just under ⅝ in) from the hem at the corner point. Secure the stitches, fold the fabric flap over and start stitching again at the other side of the point.

4. From the right side, press the edging strip away from the curtain. Fold back under by 1.5 cm (⅝ in), keeping the binding tight against the seam. Mitre the corner and pin in place.

5. Place the blind flat on to the worktable with the right side facing down. Take the pre-prepared linings and at each rod pocket carefully snip the linings so that the lining between the pockets can be unfolded.

6. Place the lining over the main fabric, pockets outwards. Carefully line up the seams and hemline. Pin the sides to hold. Secure each of the pocket stitching lines with pins at right angles to the stitching and with the pockets facing upwards. Stitch along the pocket lines, working from only one direction to avoid pulling to one side. Trim away the excess lining at the sides.

7. Pin the binding edge over the lining and slip stitch all around for a neat finish. Continue to make up the blinds following the instructions from step 6 of the Roman blinds on page 132.

DESIGN AND MAKE SOFT FURNISHINGS

DOUBLE BORDERS

Double borders give a very smart finish, especially when using fabrics in complementary colours. A second binding is added to the first binding before making up or, alternatively, a row of piping is stitched to the blind before adding the flat border.

The deepest shades of blue in the pattern have been picked out with a double border in blue and green.

1. Press a 4 cm (1½ in) strip of the contrast colour in half lengthwise. Stitch to the binding. Stitch both to the blind just inside the first line.

BINDING AN INTERLINED BLIND

1. Place the interlining flat on the worktable and smooth out any creases. Place the blind fabric over the top, right side up. Trim the interlining to the exact size of the fabric. Tack all around and pin these two fabrics together. Make up as steps 1–4 opposite, treating both fabrics as one.

2. Herringbone the binding around the blind with stitches measuring about 2 cm (¾ in).

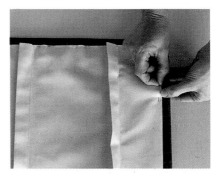

3. Place the lining over the blind, positioning the rod pockets exactly parallel to the hemline, with the lining over the binding, leaving 1.5 cm (⅝ in) showing.

HEMS AND TRIMMINGS

Roman blinds are chosen to be primarily functional but, as with all home furnishings, they should also be decorative.

Hems can be cut and made using variations of geometric forms like circles, triangles and squares. Whatever shape you decide on, check that it fits with the overall style and structure of the window frame and pane configuration. Make a paper template and pin it to the window to how it will look. Adjust the amount of shaping and scale.

1. Cut a piece of paper, card or a strip of heading buckram the width of the finished blind. Mark the centre and plan each section to be equal, making sure that one section forms the central point of the blind. Measure the strip into the required number of sections, mark the depth of the shaping at the widest and narrowest points. Use a ruler to make even shapes.

2. Cut around the shapes accurately. Pin the template to the window again to check the design and make any alterations.

3. Pin this template to the hemline of the blind fabric and cut around it, allowing 1.5 cm (⅝ in) for the seams. Cut a strip of fabric for the facing, the width of the curtain × the depth of the shaping and up to the first rod. Pin the facing to the blind, with fabrics right sides together. Stitch around the shaped edge, keeping the stitching line 1.4 cm (just under ⅝ in) from the raw edge. Trim seams to just under 1 cm (⅜ in), and snip right into the points.

4. Turn out and press into neat, even shapes. Cut a piece of buckram or other stiffening, exactly the same size as the template. Insert this against the front of the blind. Pin well to secure it in place.

5. Make up your blind following the instructions on pages 132-33. If you are using interlining, pin this carefully to the blind fabric and make up as one. The bottom batten pocket will replace the bottom rod position.

6. Stitch the batten pocket, catching in the stiffening with the lower row of stitches.

DOUBLE HEMS

It is quite fun to mix fabrics and styles with double hems. The top fabric is shaped at the hemline with a border made up and stitched behind. A plain colour will show the shaping in relief. We have made up a simple design, showing the front and back of the blind.

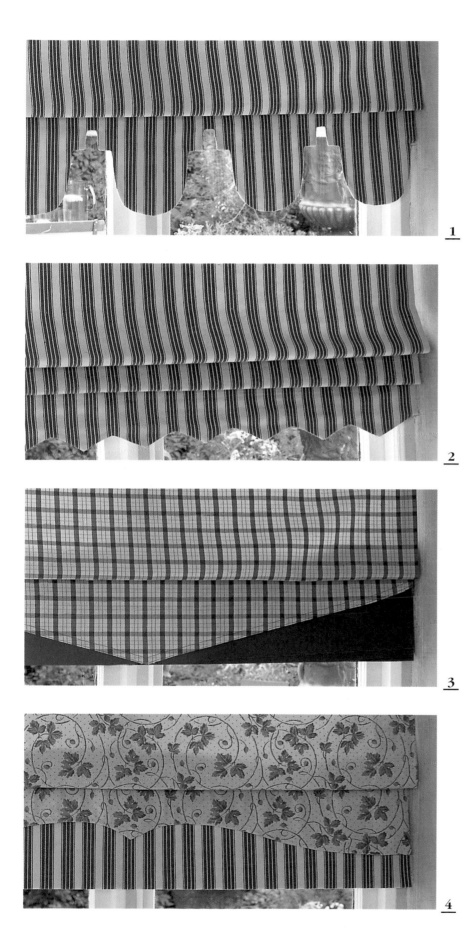

HEM IDEAS

These suggestions for hemlines show how effective attention to detail can be. You will need to choose the hem type most suited to your own decoration and room style, but use these ideas as a jumping board to experiment with materials and shapes for your own individual finish.

1. Deep shaping is only suitable when the blind will never be fully lowered, or if the blind will fall below a sill. Stunning effects can be created with rope or cord edging, fringing, contrast colours, tassels hanging from each scallop or between each shape.

2. I think this is the simplest edge shape to make. Points can be made deeper, shallower, narrower, wider, to suit any window treatment. The lower edge could be finished with piping stitched between the blind and the facing, or with cord hand stitched in place once the blind is complete.

3. A smart treatment, the blind edge could have been more heavily top stitched or made with an inset border following the diagonal lines. The dark green under skirt emphasises the shaping.

4. The combination of scallops and points should be hand drawn on to paper to make a rough template. Experiment with any combination of angular or curved geometric shapes. Mixing checks, stripes and prints in similar tones of greens and off-whites make a strong statement.

Scalloped Hems

Hemlines shaped to gently rounded or deeply curved scallops provide interesting detail, especially for fabrics printed in soft patterns as there are no sharp corners or angles to go against the flow. Pipe the edges in a small complementary check, stripe or toning plain fabric for a truly professional finish.

MAKING SCALLOPS

1. Scallops should be even in size and the best way to cut an accurate hemline is to make a template. Cut a piece of card or a strip of heading buckram the width of the blind. Mark into sections for each scallop. In addition, mark the size of the scallop at the widest and narrowest points. Draw around a household object to define the first shape. Either trace this first one and use it to copy from or continue to use the same saucer, plate or bowl. Cut out the shaped edge accurately.

2. Pin this template to the main fabric and draw around it carefully.

3. Cut the main fabric around the shaping, allowing 1.5 cm ($\frac{5}{8}$ in) for seams. Cut a strip of fabric for the facing, the width of the blind and the depth from the bottom of the scallop to the first rod/bottom batten. Pin this facing to the blind with right sides together. Pin around the scallops, then stitch slowly around each one, keeping the stitching line 1.4 cm (just under $\frac{5}{8}$ in) from the raw edge. Trim the seam to 1 cm ($\frac{3}{8}$ in) and snip right into the points. Snip the curves at approximately 1 cm ($\frac{3}{8}$ in) intervals.

4. Turn out and press into even rounded shapes. Cut a piece of facing or stiffening to the exact size of the template and insert it, to lie against the blind. Pin together. Make up the blind following the instructions on pages 132-33. The flat batten will take the place of the bottom rod. Stitch the facing over the lining to make a pocket so that the batten fits snugly. Insert the batten and slip stitch the side openings neatly together.

5. If you wish to pipe the scallops, make up enough piping for the whole job and pin around the scalloped edging on the blind fabric, 1.4 cm (just under $\frac{5}{8}$ in) from the raw edge, snipping where necessary so that the piping lies flat. Bend the piping sharply into the points and pin. Stitch around as closely to the piping as possible for a neat finish.

6. Cut a facing in the same fabric to fit from the bottom of the scallop to the top of the batten pocket. Pin to the main fabric with right sides together and stitch tight to the piping line. Trim the seam to 1 cm ($\frac{3}{8}$ in), snip as necessary, turn out and press.

Bought Edgings

The simplest Roman blind can be lifted with the addition of a bought trimming. Fringes, fan edgings, braids, tassels and gimps are available from interior decorators and furnishing fabric specialists in any combination of colours, styles and price which you could possibly want.

Choose edgings to subtly blend with the main fabric colours or to provide a complete contrast – whichever is most in keeping with the general furnishing style and fabric design. Should you really not be able to find the perfect finish, ask your interior decorator to design and organise trimmings to be made especially. This is only viable for large projects, but well worth the extra trouble if the blind is part of a larger furnishing project with curtains and pelmets.

I was very fortunate to find several pieces of hand-worked lace in an antique clothes shop. These had all probably experienced their first life attached to the sleeves and hems of night wear but I have made some feminine finishes for blinds, curtains and bed cushions.

I always like to stitch antique lace leaving the unevenness of the hand made tops showing. Simple embroidered knots hold the lace in place and suit the character of the toile de jouy – this particular one is a traditional design called 'le serment d'aimer' which roughly translates as 'the promise of love'.

Buttons and Borders

Buttons and borders provide alternative hem details, offering the chance to introduce a change of scale or a splash of colour. Experiment with checks and stripes, patterns and checks, plains in contrasting or toning colours, plains with patterns, until you find a combination which is pleasing to the eye in scale and tonal value. Buttons, eyelets, ribbons, strings, even buckles, make interesting applied details to decorate blinds.

Always remember that a detail should be just that. Whatever finish you choose must in some way enhance the window treatment and the overall room design, and not in any way push itself to the forefront to take over or detract from any other item. Remember, too, that a blind need not be made to function fully, especially if the curtains are substantial enough; it is possible to make one up as a 'half blind' to block out an unwanted and unattractive aspect.

BUTTONED AND APPLIED HEM

These blinds will be made up in exactly the same way as described on pages 132–33, with one adaptation – the bottom batten will be fitted in the position of the bottom rod instead of the base of the blind. When you calculate the rod positions, remember to make allowance for the decorative hem detail to hang well below the folds when the blind is raised. An attached hem should add weight and be heavy enough in its own right not to curl and buckle. You might need to slip a length of chain weight along the bottom of the hem if the fabric does not hang as well as you would like.

MAKING UP

1. Make up blind following the instructions on pages 132–33, leaving the fabrics free at the hemline.

2. Cut a strip of another fabric the width of the blind, plus 2 cm (¾ in) at each side for the seams × 4 times the finished depth. Press this piece of fabric in half lengthwise, right sides inside. Open out and press each side to the centre. Open out and pin three sides together and make 1.8 cm (just under ¾ in) seams on both short sides.

3. Trim across the corner and trim the seam to 1 cm (⅜ in).

4. Turn out and press. Fold the fabric to the inside along the previously pressed lines.

5. Check the depth of the lowest section of the blind and trim the hemline so that all layers are level. Stitch along the lower edge to hold the fabrics together.

6. Sleeve the folded fabric over and pin in position. Attach to the main fabric with buttons or other type of applied decoration, making sure that the stitching goes right through to hold the applied hem firmly in place.

1. A denim border contrasts with unbleached artists' linen used for the main blind and fastened with men's coat buttons. Any decorative buttoning could be used and the fabrics could be plain with a pattern, a check with a stripe.

2. Attach tabs of fabric or tape and a contrast fabric to the blind hem. Stitch the raw edges together to secure and sandwich into the folded denim. Fabric-covered buttons add the finishing touch.

3. I suppose this hem is attached rather than applied but is still relevant to the purpose of considering what other hem options might be possible. The blind hem needed to be finished and a narrow batten inserted for weight. Follow the instructions given to make the shaped edge for the 'applied hem'. Slip stitch the top edge together. Make holes and fit eyelets as shown in the kit instructions and thread through cord, knotting the ends.

4. Another way to use a scalloped edge. Cut the shapes and make up the blind hem with piping as shown on page 138. Make up the applied hem as shown, but instead of sleeving it over, slide it under the scalloped edge and hand-stitch the scallops to the hem, making small and neat stitches between the main fabric and the piping.

AUSTRIAN
BLINDS

Austrian blinds are more correctly pull-up curtains. The fullness is across the width, but the fabric is cut to be overlong, leaving the bottom 30 cm (12 in) or so in folds which drape in swags according to the amount of fullness allowed.

The blinds can be made very full if lightweight fabrics are used, but sides and hems should not be over-filled. Instead, finish with a trimming or hand stitching.

In the blind above pleated headings at each scallop add just enough fullness for soft drapes, but do not detract from the pattern on the fabric: it still remains as a picture.

The scarlet blind on the right demonstrates how gathers bring out the best qualities of a plain fabric as the light and shadow play on the folds, enriching the colour and weave.

Austrian blinds can be made with little or much fullness, depending how you want them to look. Use lightweight silks or cottons for a really opulent effect, heavier-weight cottons or wools for a more formal look. Decide on the shape you are looking for and follow the instructions on page 181 to estimate the amount of fabric and edgings you will need to order.

MAKING UP

1. Place the blind fabric right side facing down on to the worktable. Turn over the sides and hem by 10 cm (4 in) and pin to hold. Mitre the corner as explained on page 8, and herringbone the sides and hem in place.

2. Place the lining on the blind fabrics, matching the seams. Lock stitch the seams together.

3. Fold the lining over along the stitched raw edge and trim 4 cm (1½ in) in from trim line. Turn under 2 cm (¾ in) and pin, leaving 8 cm (3¼ in) of the main fabric showing all round.

4. Slip stitch all round and press lightly. Measuring from the bottom upwards, and at 30 cm (12 in) intervals across the blind, mark the overall drop. Fold the fabric and lining over along the overall drop line and pin.

5. Mark the ring positions following your original plan. Always measure each one from the bottom of the blind upwards to avoid any errors. The outer row will be on the lining edge and the others at equal intervals between. It is always best to make one row along each seam line. Allow an average spacing of 10–20 cm (4–8 in) between each ring.

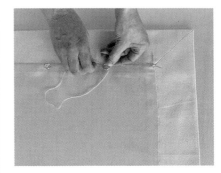

6. Gather up the blind in your hands and test how close together the gathers should be for your window. Stitch each ring into the lining two or three times, pick up threads from the front, stitch again into the lining, wind the thread round and double stitch to fasten off securely.

7. Thread the cords through from the bottom ring upwards, knotting and stitching the cords together at the lowest ring. Trim the heading as necessary.

MAKING UP HEADINGS

1. For a gathered heading, fold over 5-7 cm (2-3 in) and pin gathering tape to cover the raw edge. Stitch, then pull up to the finished width. Cut a strip of lining the length of the finished width plus 4 cm (1½ in) for turnings and three times the depth of the tape. Stitch fastening tape to the centre. Press the two sides under to make a band just wider than the tape. Slip stitch the band securely covering the heading tape.

2. For a pleated heading, trim the fabric and lining to double the depth of the required pleats above the overall drop line. Fold under double and pin. Slip stitch the open sides down. Mark the gap and pleat widths along the top of the blind. Stitch each pleat, press and stitch down.

Fan-edged braid adds shape and colour to a frilled edge, and a gathered heading is made more interesting with knotted cords in the same tones. Some braids have a decorative top so these might be better stitched to the front of the blind. A fan-edged braid with a plain top should be stitched on before the frill and sandwiched between the fabric and the lining.

HEMS AND HEADINGS

Much of the character of an Austrian blind is determined by the fullness and the manner in which this fullness is contained at the heading and decorated at the hem. The heading can be pleated, gathered or trimmed with ribbon or braid, while the hemline might be kept plain, bordered with a contrast fabric, frilled or decorated with bought trimmings.

1. Austrian blinds will hang more evenly if the hemline is weighted in some way. The degree of weight needed should be considered with the size of the blind. A heavy fabric will warrant a deep bullion fringe, whereas a light fabric can be weighted effectively with a light linen or silk fringe. Trimmings made with similar combinations of colours to those of the main fabric, such as these here, add detail which is subtle and often more compatible with the overall room scheme than a simple contrasting colour. The formal lines dictated by the strong stripes are contained within a discreet pleated heading.
2. Austrian blinds are in themselves full enough for the fabric to be greatly enriched with the light and shadow play of the horizontal and vertical gathers. Adding more frills will more often than not detract from the whole point of making an Austrian blind. Sometimes you see blinds with the sides and hem all frilled. These blinds can be rather

overpowering, so take care of the size and fullness of the frilled edging. A deeply frilled hem is perhaps best, giving enough additional weight to the blind and added interest. Just one-and-a-half times fullness prevents the frill becoming too dominant and the ribbon edging strengthens the style. The simple gathered heading has also been finished with a row of ribbed ribbon.

3. Blanket stitch is probably the one stitch which every child learns to sew during the first few school years. It is very simple and easy to learn, but very effective. Use a thickness of thread suited to the main fabric; here, we used a medium weight wool for the heavy cotton and a stitch size proportionate with the blind size and the strength of the fabric. Threading the heading on to a

pole is an effective treatment, no matter how much fullness has been included. Stitch a casing which measures half the circumference of the pole plus a little extra for ease, about 5 cm (2 in) from the top of the blind. Thread the pole through the casing, gathering the fabric evenly. The fixing batten needs to be fitted to the wall immediately below the pole.

FESTOON BLINDS

Use silks and organzas for very feminine blinds, as on the left.

MAKING UP

1. Place the fabric on to the worktable, right side facing down. Turn in the sides 7 cm (3 in) and press.

2. Cut strips of fabric 15 cm (6 in) wide and twice the width of the blind, and join together. Fold in half lengthwise and run a gathering thread 1.5 cm (⅝ in) from the raw edge.

3. Divide the blind into ten sections and mark each with a marking tack. Repeat with the frill.

4. Unpick the thread 3 cm (1¼ in) from each end of the frill and stitch half of the frill to the blind, with the folded edge against the 6 cm (2¼ in) side fold as shown. Snip the blind 1.5 cm (⅝ in) to meet the edge of the frill.

5. Pull up the gathering threads. Pin the corresponding marking tacks together and distribute gathers evenly between.

6. Fold the sides over again and herringbone all around the sides and the hem to hold them in place. Slip stitch the edge of the frill to enclose the raw edges.

7. Place the blind back on to the worktable, right side down and place the lining over, matching the seams. Score the lining along the folded edge and trim the lining away 4 cm (1½ in) from this line.

> The fabric can be cut up to 200 per cent wider and 300 per cent longer than the window for a really opulent effect.

8. Slip stitch the lining along the frill to enclose all raw edges.

9. Pin narrow blind tape to cover the lining raw edge, on each seam, and as many times across each width as planned. Pull out the cord so it remains free of the heading tape and tuck the ends of the tapes underneath.

10. Pull up the heading tape and the vertical tapes. Thread cords through from bottom to top, knotting and stitching the ends.

CURTAINS

Curtains can be dramatic or subtle, luxurious or informal, decorative or plain. Before you start to make them, take time to consider the effect you want to create. Unlined curtains are ideal for summer and, simpler to make than lined ones, they can be just as effective. Interlined curtains will fall generously and can be dressed in formal folds or informal gathers. Contrasting linings add an element of surprise to the design of a room.

Simple ideas using fabrics in a stylish way are often the most effective. Here the simple gingham check opens to reveal fabric which would usually have been used for the front.

The type of heading you use will depend on a number of factors: the size of the window, the style of the window treatment, whether the curtains need to be well stacked back, and whether they can be more decorative than practical. Gathers suit informal curtaining as headings may be tied and buttoned to poles and rings. Tabbed headings are smart alternatives and give a lovely decorative finish – but their use must be restricted to windows where the curtain pole is easily reached as they have to be pulled back by hand. Headings can be finished with an almost infinite variety of detail including frills and ribbons, scallops and piping.

If you want to mix and match colours, textures and patterns but are unsure about how to do this, stay with the ones with which you feel most comfortable, but approach them in a new way. Collect scraps of fabrics and coloured papers, study books and magazines so that you can begin to understand just how colours work together and how you could use different combinations of patterns and textures.

UNLINED CURTAINS

Unlined curtains are the simplest form of window covering to make and, with careful preparation and well chosen fabric, your curtains can look as good as any more complicated design. For those new to curtain-making, this is the place to start. If you need to make something quickly or perhaps find yourself on a very tight budget, unlined curtains using inexpensive fabrics but with plenty of fullness will make effective and very rewarding window treatments. I often use unlined curtains as draw curtains for the summer, allowing the sunlight to filter through while the heavier winter curtains are draped up to the sides.

Use silks, muslins, calicoes, and experiment with ribbons, braids, cords, ties, buttons and motifs to produce your own personalised finish. Turn to page 165 to see how very good sheers and layered curtains can look.

Change heavy winter curtains to simple unlined cotton for the summer months. Crisp blue and white edging defines these white curtains and coordinating tablecloth.

DESIGN AND MAKE SOFT FURNISHINGS

MAKING UP

1. Place the cut and joined fabric for one curtain on to the worktable, with the right side facing down, lining up the hem and one side with two edges of the table. Smooth the fabric out, sweeping the edge of a metre rule or yardstick across the table and press to remove any creases. Turn in the side edge by 6 cm (2¼ in) using a small measuring gauge to make sure that the turning is even. Press lightly. Fold in half to give a 3 cm (1⅛ in) double turning. Pin and press again. Turn up the hem by 10 cm (4 in). Press lightly, then fold in half to make a 5 cm (2 in) double hem. Pin and press.

2. For medium to heavyweight fabrics, mitre the corner as shown here and described more fully on page 8.

3. Stitch both the sides and the hem with neat slip stitches, 1.5-2 cm (⅝-¾ in) in length. Ladder stitch the corner, slipping in a fabric-covered weight.

4. For sheer and lightweight fabrics, fold the sides and hems over so that the layers are exactly on top of each other, and slip stitch along the fold so that the stitches are almost invisible.

5. Measure from the hem to the top of the curtain to mark the hook drop of the finished curtain. If you do not yet have the exact measurements because the fittings are not in place, mark the estimated position. Measure at 30 cm (12 in) intervals and pin a line across the curtain. If you know the overall drop also mark this line with a row of pins.

6. Carefully move the curtain across the table and repeat with the other side.

7. Sheer, unlined curtains which will be used in doorways or open windows will need to be weighted along the hems to prevent them flapping about in any breeze. Insert a length of fabric-covered chain weight (see page 11) into the hem.

8. An attractive alternative to step 7 is to stitch several rows of decorative stitching to give the required weight and substance to the curtain hem.

LINED CURTAINS

The purpose of lining curtains is twofold – firstly, to protect the principal fabric from exposure to sunlight and/or the effects of condensation which will eventually cause fading and rotting, and secondly to add bulk.

Cotton sateen lining is available in three basic shades – ecru, cream and white, and in various qualities. A specialist furnishing fabric supplier will also be able to offer you coloured linings so that you can tone your lining with the main fabric. Lining fabric is relatively inexpensive and my advice is always to buy the best lining possible. If you look at several different qualities, you will immediately see the difference in the weight of yarn and quality of weave, and realise that saving costs on the lining fabric will be a false economy.

It is important that the lining you choose has been treated to withstand strong sunlight and dampness. However, while good curtain fabric will last for many years, linings should be replaced completely every 10–15 years. A window with a sunny aspect will need more linings and curtains than a north-facing window. Once a year, check the linings and replace the leading edge as soon as it starts to wear.

Lining curtains adds body as well as protecting the main fabric from the effects of strong sunlight or dampness. Over-sized gathered headings flop over informally.

DESIGN AND MAKE SOFT FURNISHINGS

MAKING UP

1. Place the fabric for one curtain on the worktable with the right side facing down, lining up the hem and one long side to two edges of the table. Smooth out the fabric and press to remove any creases. Turn in the side seams by 6 cm (2¼ in), using a small measuring gauge to make sure that the turning is even. Pin every 12–15 cm (4¾–6 in) and press. Turn up the hem by 16 cm (6½ in), checking that the pattern runs evenly across the width, and press lightly. Open out the fold and refold in half, to make an 8 cm (3¼ in) double hem. Pin and press.

2. Mitre the corners as shown here and described more fully on page 8. Make an angled mitre so that the hem and the side match along the diagonal.

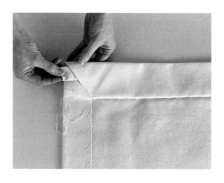

3. Stitch the length of the side with herringbone stitches, approximately 5 cm (2 in) in length. Picking up only one thread at a time, slip stitch the hem, stitching a weight into each seam. Ladder stitch the mitre, slipping a weight into the corner.

4. Place the pre-prepared curtain lining (see page 14) on top of the curtain, wrong sides together, matching the seam lines and placing the top of the lining hem exactly on top of the curtain hem.

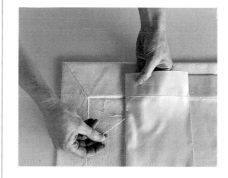

5. Turn back the lining and lock stitch to secure the lining twice across each width at equal distances and at all seams, using the same colour thread as the lining fabric. Reposition the lining and smooth out the creases.

6. Using scissors, score the lining along the folded edge of the curtain. Trim along this line. Turn the raw edge under leaving 3 cm (1¼ in) of curtain showing. Pin and stitch the edges of the curtain beginning 4 cm (1½ in) from the bottom corner and continuing until just below the heading.

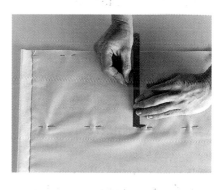

7. Measure from the hem to the top of the curtain and mark the hook drop of the finished curtain. If you cannot be exact because the fittings are not in place, mark the estimated position. Measure across the curtain at 30 cm (12 in) intervals and pin through both layers along the hook drop line. Mark the overall drop line with pins.

8. Fold the side to the middle and move the curtain across the table. Make up the other side in the same way.

INTERLINED CURTAINS

Interlined curtains provide warmth and look luxurious.

1. Place the fabric on the work-table, the right side facing down. Align the hem and one long side to two edges of the table. Smooth the fabric out and clamp it to the table at 60 cm (24 in) intervals. Put the interlining on top; line up the seams and smooth out.

2. The interlining must now be locked to the main fabric at each seam and twice between each seam. Fold the interlining back on itself at the first seam and lock stitch all the way down using double thread. Stitch close to the hem but stop just short of the hook drop. Fold the interlining back flat, smooth out and then fold two thirds back again. Repeat the lock stitch for the whole length and again on the third of the width.

Your curtain is likely to be wider than your table; however, as interlined curtains should not be moved until they are stitched together, you must finish this part of the curtain before moving the other half on to the table.

3. Trim the interlining if necessary so that the sides of both the main fabric and the interlining are even. Remove the side clamps and turn back both fabric and interlining by 6 cm (2¼ in), using a small measuring gauge to make sure that the turning is even. With the tips of your fingers, check that the interlining is well tucked into the fold and a solid, firm edge is pinned in place. (A soft fabric might require the interlining to be locked to the main fabric along the folded edge. Use small stitches and make sure that they do not pull on the fabric at all.)

Trim the interlining along the hem if necessary and fold it up by 12 cm (4¾ in). Press lightly and pin securely.

4. Mitre the bottom corner following the instructions on page 8. Make a long mitre so that the 12 cm (4¾ in) hem and the 6 cm (2¼ in) side match along the diagonal. If you are using very heavy interlining with heavy fabric you might need to cut away the bulk of the interlining. Open out the mitre and trim along the folded diagonal line.

5. Stitch along the length of the side with long stitches approximately 5 cm (2 in) in length as shown on page 6 and along the hem with 2 cm (¾ in) herringbone stitches. Catch both layers of interlining but do not go through to the front fabric. Insert a weight into the mitre opening and ladder stitch to close with small, neat stitches.

6. Clamp the curtain back on to the table. Place the lining over the interlining, matching up the seam lines and allowing the lining to overhang the hem by approximately 10 cm (4 in). Smooth out with the ruler and lock the lining to the interlining along the same lines that hold the interlining to the main fabric. Start at the hemline and finish just before the hook drop.

7. With the point of the scissors, score the lining along the folded edge and trim to this line. Fold under the raw edge, leaving 3 cm (1¼ in) of the curtain fabric showing. Pin to secure. Trim the hem of the lining so that it is exactly 10 cm (4 in) longer than the curtain. Pin the lower, raw edge to the hem fold and take up the excess fabric by finger pressing a tuck into the lining along the stitched hemline. Press this fold downwards and pin to hold it in place. Fold the raw edge of the lining under so that the fold is 4 cm (1½ in) from the hem. Pin. Slip stitch the sides and hem from the hook drop to the edge of the table.

8. At this stage, measure from the hem to the top of the curtain to mark the hook drop of the finished curtain. If you do not yet have the exact measurement because fittings are not in place, mark the estimated position. Measure across the curtain at 30 cm (12 in) intervals and pin through all three layers at the hook drop measurement, to secure. Pin two or three more times between each of these to make a definite line.

9. Remove the clamps and carefully lift the curtain along the table. You should ask for some help to do this, so that the fabrics are disturbed as little as possible.

Re-clamp the other side of the curtain to the table. Continue smoothing the interlining against the main fabric, folding it back and locking in as before. Mark the hook drop all along to line up with the other side.

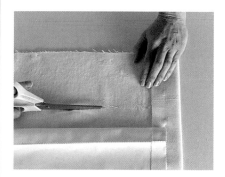

10. Check the exact overall drop measurements and mark with pins accordingly. Fold the lining back on itself along the pinned line. Remove the pins and carefully cut away the interlining along this line. Pin again to secure. Herringbone stitch the interlining to the curtain. Fold the main fabric over with the lining and continue with your chosen heading.

OVERLONG CURTAINS

The choice of curtain hem length is a purely personal one, however I usually advise and make curtains just 2–3 cm (¾–1¼ in) longer than floor length so that the fabric just bumps the floor. The reasons for this are several. Firstly, curtain fabric can drop or pull back in the time between making up and hanging, thus making it very difficult for an amateur to gauge an exact length. Secondly, very few window tops are parallel to the floor and overlong curtains make this variation less obvious. Old houses will almost always have draughts from around the window frame and below the skirting boards, which overlong curtains take up. And last, but by no means least, I *like* the look of curtains which just fall to the floor.

HEADINGS

Curtain headings can be gathered, bunched, or tabbed and tied.

GATHERED HEADINGS

These may be frills created by stitching on standard hook tape and pulling on the cords, or they may be finished with a variety of details. A 6–8 cm (2¼–3¼ in) frill is ideal with a pole fitting. Adjust this as necessary in order to suit the curtain fitting which you have chosen.

For a 6 cm (2¼ in) frill you should allow 12 cm (4¼ in) plus 1.5 cm (⅝ in) to go under the tape. Cut away excess fabric.

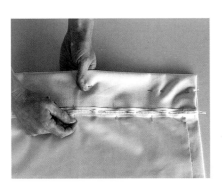

1. If your curtain is interlined, fold the lining back and trim away the interlining at the overall drop line. Fold fabric and lining over, pin on the tape and stitch close to the outer edges, always stitching with the heading towards the body of the machine. Pull the heading up to the required size and gather evenly across the width.

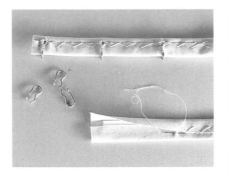

2. Make a hook band. Cut a piece of heading tape or heading buckram the width of the tape and of length equal to the finished heading size. Cut a strip of fabric three times this width and 4 cm (1½ in) longer. Fold the fabric over the band, trimming and herringboning the raw edge. Position hooks at the leading edge, at the return and at 11–13 cm (4¼–5 in) intervals across the width. Stitch securely to the back of the band to cover the tape.

3. Slipstitch the hook band neatly to cover the heading tape.

HAND GATHERED

1. Check your overall drop measurement and adjust pins accordingly. Fold the lining back and trim away the interlining, if used, along the overall drop line. Trim fabric and lining 7.5 cm (3 in) from this line and press to the back. Experiment with different stitch lengths to determine the stitch length you will need to obtain your required pleat size.

2. Divide the heading into 10 sections and mark each with a coloured tack. Make one row of stitches 3 cm (1¼ in) from the folded edge. Make a parallel row 3 cm (1¼ in) from the first. Pull up the two threads together evenly.

3. Make a hook band; divide into sections and match to the heading. Even out gathers, pin and slip stitch.

The binding for headings should be taken from a mid-tone in the fabric.

1. Tied and gathered: As an alternative to hooks, a pretty gathered or pleated heading might be tied to the pole or to curtain rings. Ties could be short and tied into a neat bow, or long and trailing. Plan the number of ties to be about 11–15 cm (4¼–6 in) apart and to suit the pole width. Divide the curtain by this number of gaps between ties and mark the tie positions. Make ties as on page 8 and pin under the tape. Secure each tie with double stitches as the tape is being stitched in place.

2. Scalloped frill: Check your overall drop and hook drop and adjust the pins accordingly. Make a scalloped template, pin this shaped edge along the overall drop line and cut around it through all layers. Using the same template, cut a facing from a strip of main fabric the length of the heading × the frill depth, plus 1.5 cm (⅝ in) to fit under the tape. Make up enough piping (see page 9) and stitch around the scallops. Pin the facing on with right sides together and stitch just

1

2

3

4

inside the previous stitching line. Trim, snipping into the corners. Press the scallops to shape. Pin and stitch the tape in place and cover with a hook band.

3. Adding ribbon: Check your overall drop and hook drop and adjust the pins accordingly. Add the frill depth plus 1.5 cm (⅝ in) to go under the tape and trim away all excess fabric. Trim away interlining along the overall drop line. Fold over the main fabric and lining and press. Turn the curtain to the front and position the ribbon so that it will finish just 1 cm (⅜ in) from the frill fold. Pin to the fabric only and stitch along both sides. Fold the frill over again and stitch tape to the hook drop measurement. Pull up, spreading gathers evenly and attach the hook band.

4. Pocket headings: Pocket or slot headings allow curtains to be threaded directly on to the pole or wire. They are often used for voiles and sheers and for curtains with a fixed heading which open on to ties or holdbacks rather than being pulled open and closed in the conventional manner. Allow 8–12 cm (3¼–4¾ in) for a curtain frill and 2 cm (¾ in) for voiles above the pocket.

Check your overall drop and trim away any interlining along this line. Add the frill return and twice the pocket depth, and trim away any excess fabric. (To find the pocket depth, add 10 per cent to the circumference of your pole for easement and divide in half.) Fold under, pin and then stitch along both the fold line and the stitching line which will become the top of the pocket.

BUNCHED

Bunched headings are very effective and extremely simple to make. And you can achieve very different looks using this same technique. For example, silk curtains finished with bunched headings look extremely sophisticated, yet heavy linen curtains will look very relaxed and have more of a country style.

Fine fabrics can be bunched successfully if at least three times the fullness of fabric has been used. Insert a length of scrunched organdie or fine net into the heading after the tape has been stitched on to give the curtain body and to help the folds fall correctly.

All interlined curtains make suitable candidates for bunched headings, but if medium or lightweight interlining has been used, insert a double layer into the heading before bunching.

Check the overall drop and hook drop, adjust the pins accordingly. Add the frill depth plus 1.5 cm (⅝ in) to go under the tape and cut away any excess fabric. Trim the interlining back another 2 cm (¾ in). Fold the heading down to the hook drop line, pin and stitch 3 cm (1¼ in) deep tape in place. Pull up and stitch on the hook band.

Turn the curtain to the front and bunch up the heading with your fingers. Using a long needle and double thread secure through the folds and into the back as often as needed to hold the shape without squashing the folds. Sew up the open ends by hand, gathering slightly.

Gathered headings are scrunched up and stitched in place. Hanging from a painted pole, they add an informal finish to these interlined curtains.

Tabbed and Tied Headings

I used a little spare fabric to make alternately coloured tabs and buttons for a checkerboard effect; bought tapes or ribbons could be substituted if your time is limited. Most fabrics respond well to contrasting detail; striped and checked fabrics worked together, with perhaps a plain tone to add definition, are especially rewarding.

None of these headings is difficult to make if you have basic skills and like to experiment with cords, eyelets, ribbons, and even string, to create an individual finish. Some of the headings will not allow the curtains to be pulled back as far as you might wish, but they are ideal for decorative and fixed curtains. Most will allow the curtain to take up little space when pulled back, especially those threaded on to poles through large eyelets.

Always stiffen the headings with buckram, cotton heading tape or dressmakers' interfacing, to prevent the fabric flopping and looking untidy. Hand or machine stitch between the fabric and lining before binding, or insert into a folded heading. Unlined curtains will need a facing to cover the stiffening.

MAKING UP

1. Make fabric tabs in any size, but usually 2–4 cm (¾–1½ in) wide and long enough to fit easily over your pole. Allow enough for buttoning to the front and fixing to the back. Stitch securely to the curtain heading just beyond the overall drop before turning the heading over.

2. Stitch buttons to the front, securing them right through all layers of fabric. Use strong buttonhole thread to make sure that the tabs are secure, as this stitching will be holding the full weight of the curtain.

1. Add a 5 cm (2 in) border to the top of the curtain and stiffen it with heading buckram. Fit 20 mm (¾ in) eyelets to thread on to a 15 mm (⅝ in) pole.

2. Add 10 cm (4 in) to the overall drop, fold this in half and insert a 5 cm (2 in) band of stiffening; slip stitch along the fold. Punch 10 mm (⅜ in) eyelets and thread through double cords.

3. Add a 5 cm (2 in) border to the top of the curtain and stiffen with heading buckram. Fit 20 mm (¾ in) eyelets and 30 cm (12 in) ribbons to tie to the pole with little half bows.

4. Bind the curtain all round, stitching in 5 cm (2 in) of interfacing into the heading. Make ties measuring 1 × 45 cm (⅜ × 18 in). Stitch into the binding at regular intervals and tie to the curtain rings.

5. Bind the curtain all round, inserting 5 cm (2 in) soft interfacing into the heading. Cut tabs and bind these to match. Secure to the back of the heading and hold the front with a button.

6. Bind the curtain all round, inserting a soft interfacing into the heading. Stitch 100 cm (40 in) ties into the headings at intervals. Loop over the pole and tie in bows.

7. Add 10 cm (4 in) to the overall drop, fold in half, inserting a 5 cm (2 in) stiffening. Stitch 45 × 5 cm (18 × 2 in) piped tabs at regular intervals, loop over the pole and tie into half bows. Stitch in place.

8. Make a stiffened band with a shaped lower edge, the finished width of the curtain. Gather the curtain on to the band. Stitch ribbon loops, fold the band over and decorate with bought motifs.

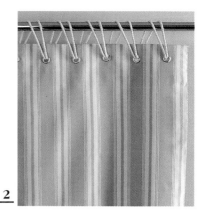

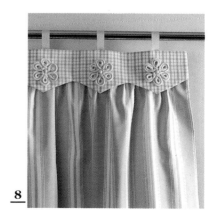

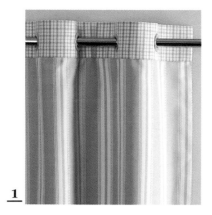

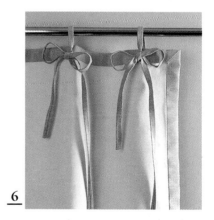

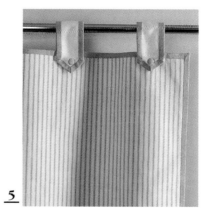

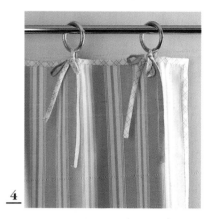

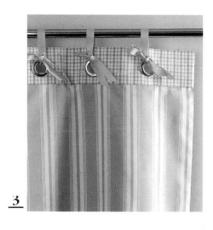

USING FABRICS

To allow maximum light into a room choose curtains made from sheers. These encompass unlined and semi-transparent curtaining which, although decorative, is chosen and fitted for protection of some sort. Fabrics include muslins, very fine calicoes, organdie, silks, fine linens, linen scrim, lace and cotton voile. Any that you use should be easy to clean and should not react to sudden changes in temperature. Some linens and cottons – usually white, cream or off white – can be bought unbleached and muslins, silks and voiles will all dye easily. The curtains must be very full if the fabric is to be shown at its best.

If you want more privacy than sheer curtains will give you, go for fabrics like brocades and damasks, gingham and ticking, velvet and cambric. Each of these will add its own special touch – formal or informal – to a room.

You can mix and match a sheer and heavier fabric – fine linen with a jute scrim undercurtain, for example – or combine sheers of different colours, as on the right. Curtains lined with a contrasting fabric are also effective.

Finally, use scraps of leftover fabric to good effect: for tiebacks, as on the left, or for bows, roses, rouleaux and simple ties.

1. Yellow ochre, tan and red layers combine for an exotic effect. The headings of the top two layers were cut into deep scallops and edged with narrow ribbon in complementary colours. By tying each layer back individually, the colours can be seen in their own right and with added depths.

2. The whole scheme for this room was designed from the hand-printed olive leaf chosen for a half blind. Half blinds which pull up and down only a little way are very useful when the outlook from just the top half of a window needs to be obscured. The checked and buttoned edge was later picked up in the sofas and cushions.

The excellent quality of the cloth used for the blind, and the printing technique with its simple design, set a style which I was keen to keep in my interpretation. The walls were coloured and

stencil printed not to copy but to echo the olive leaf design. Two very different linens were chosen for the drapes to reflect the spirit of 'elegant naivete'. The sheers were made from very inexpensive jute scrim and the curtains were made of the best quality linen, sewn with oversized pin tucks and all hand embroidered in feather stitch using perlé thread with a slight sheen which contrasts beautifully and subtly with the matt linen weave.

CONTRAST LININGS

When choosing a contrasting fabric for lining curtains it is best to use simple stripes or two-coloured small prints which add

to the design, rather than a plain colour which may be too strong viewed from outside – and would make too much of a statement.

Where the linings are intended to be on show, the edges need to be finished neatly. One way to do this is to finish the edge with cord or piping. This piping (above left) was chosen to pick up the main greeny blue colour, stitched to the lining before making up. Checks

and stripes always make pleasing combinations. Richly coloured curtains in browns and reds are bordered in a plain caramel and lined with a terracotta stripe (above right). The interlining is locked to the curtain fabric and the lining to the interlining before the binding is stitched on. The binding strips are pinned to the front and stitched on, through all layers, pressed, folded to the back

and hand stitched to cover the stitching line. The instructions on page 9 for binding edgings will help you. Before you take the curtain off the worktable, pin all around at about 5 cm (2 in) intervals with the pins at right angles to the edges. These pins will remain in place while the binding is stitched on, keeping the fabrics together and the lining straight.

Door curtains are often seen from both sides, in which case equal attention needs to be given to both fabrics. Fabrics that are very similar in weight and coordinate as perfectly as these do, look stunning, but you could use lighter and darker colourings and, with the right headings, make the curtain reversible for winter and summer.

MAKING UP

Neatening the edge

If curtains are equally valid from both sides, as in the case of room dividers, bed curtains and door curtains, each fabric should be stitched together right on the edge to create a neat finish. Stitching piping, cording, or fringing to either side neatens the edge and provides an anchor against which to stitch the other side.

Adding piping

A piped edge stitched to the lining before making up gives a firm line to stitch against and looks impressive.

Cut linings 3 cm (1¼ in) smaller all round than the flat curtain. Stitch piping to the sides and hem, place lining on to the curtain, lock in and stitch to the main fabric with small, neat running stitches through the back of the piping.

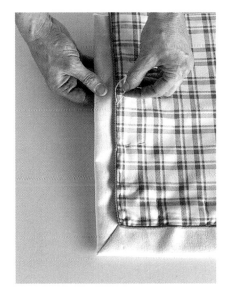

Patterned lining

Using a plain fabric on the front of a curtain and a patterned one on the inside can be very effective. To achieve this, the headings must remain in position while the curtains are held back. This lets the light shine through to show up the patterned lining.

Take the lining around to the front to make a narrow binding. Mitre the corner, as shown. Slip stitch the binding in place, just catching a thread from the lining side of the curtain.

TIEBACKS

MAKING A SASH

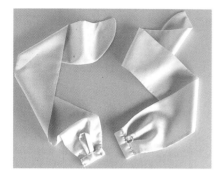

To establish the length of the sash, drape a length of scrap fabric around your curtain, trim to size, tie a bow or knot to the front or side of the curtain, pin in position and mark where the rings should be stitched to fit the tieback hook.

Cut fabric the length and twice the width of your template, fold in half with right sides together and stitch from each end to the centre, leaving a 12 cm (4¾ in) gap. Trim the seams back to 5 mm (¼ in), turn through, press and slip stitch the opening. Cut this length into two as shown, turn under the raw edges and pleat the sash ends to approximately 3 cm (1¼ in). Stitch to neaten and stitch a ring just inside one end and a fabric loop in the other. Fit on to the hook and tie into a bow or knot. Stitch so that the bow or knot cannot easily be undone.

Large bows and sashes for feminine window treatments can be made simply and quickly or in much more detail with contrast linings, pipings and ribbons.

MAKING A BOW

To make this bow, cut two pieces of fabric 45 × 12 cm (18 × 4¾ in) and piping to go all round. Stitch the piping to the right side of one piece, very close to the piping stitching line. Place the other piece of fabric over the top, pin carefully in place and stitch from the first side, keeping your stitching line just inside the last one. Leave a 12 cm (4¾ in) gap in the middle. Trim the seams to 5 mm (¼ in) and turn right side out. Pull the corners out with a pin and press along the seam line. Slip stitch the gap, pin the bow to the worktable and tie. Stitch the bow in position so that no one can come along and untie your beautiful creation.

MAKING A ROSE

Use different lengths and widths of fabric for different sized roses and buds. For this rose, cut one piece of fabric 1 m (1 yd) long, making it 14 cm (5½ in) at one end and 10 cm (4 in) at the other. Fold in half lengthwise and run a hand-stitched gathering thread 1.5 cm (⅝ in) in from the raw edges. Pull up to 50 cm (20 in) and, starting at the narrow end, roll up to make the rose, keeping the raw edges tight together. Stitch through all layers to hold the shape, cut a small square of fabric and stitch to the back to cover the frayed ends.

TIES

Simple ties also make very effective tiebacks, again for informal rooms. Tie a piece of tape or an offcut of fabric around your curtain to determine the length and width and follow the instructions on page 8. Checks and stripes can be bought inexpensively and are most effective used on the cross or in complementary colours and different weaves.

ROULEAUX

To make a rouleau measuring 45 × 6 cm (18 × 2¼ in) cut a strip of fabric 50 × 14 cm (20 × 5½ in) and a piece of polyester wadding 50 × 70 cm (20 × 28 in). Roll up the wadding and loosely herringbone. Press under 1.5 cm (⅝ in) along one length. Fold this strip over the wadding roll, pin the folded edge over the raw edge and slip stitch. Cut two small pieces to stitch over the ends, with a ring at one end and a fabric loop at the other.

A rouleau tieback (above) is decorative and is finished with rose in the same fabric. Below: the simplest treatments are so often the most effective.

BINDINGS AND BORDERS

Adding bindings and borders to curtains gives you the opportunity to experiment with different colours and textures. Borders may be wide, narrow, on the edge, or set in from the edge, and on as many sides of the curtain as you wish. Double and triple borders take time and need very accurate cutting and stitching but are always most effective. Try using one or two plain colours set into a pattern.

The really important factor to consider is that the fabrics must be of similar quality and content. It would be such a shame to spend time choosing and making to find the fabrics reacting differently to room temperature and pulling against each other. So a matt finish may be used with a sheen, pattern with plain, stripe with pattern, as long as the fibre content is the same and the weave similar.

Attention to the detailed finish of any curtain will optimise the hard work that you have put into making them so far.

MAKING BOUND EDGES

My standard edging size is 1.5 cm (⅝ in). I often adjust this a fraction either way, slightly more for a larger curtain or a deeper frill, and less for a dark colour or smaller frill. Order edging fabric to be at least as long as your curtains, so that the strips can be cut the length of the roll, entailing as few joins as possible, with none at all on the leading edge.

EDGING AN UNLINED CURTAIN

1. Cut and join enough strips of fabric 6 cm (2¼ in) wide to bind all edges.

2. Place the curtain flat on to the worktable with the wrong side facing down. Pin the edging strip along the leading edge as shown. Stop pinning 1.5 cm (⅝ in) from the corner. Fold the edging over at a right angle and continue pinning along the hemline.

3. Stitch along the leading edge at exactly 1.4 cm (just under ⅝ in) from the raw edges. Stop stitching 1.5 cm (⅝ in) from the hem edge at the corner point. Fold the flap over and start stitching again at the other side of the flap, checking that the needle is inserted next to the last stitch.

These simple curtains made from ticking have been bound on all four edges with a deep yellow cotton to echo the colours of the ties and window seat.

4. From the right side, press the edging strip away from the curtain. Fold back under 1.5 cm (⅝ in), folding the edging tight against the seam, mitre the corner.

5. Turn the fabric over to the back. Mitre the corner by first folding the free side to the curtain edge and over again to enclose the raw edges. Snip the adjacent binding strip towards the corner, and fold the next length of binding over as before. Pin to hold in place. Slip stitch every 1 cm (⅜ in), picking up a machine stitch as you go so that no stitches are visible from the front.

BINDING A LINED CURTAIN

Follow the method above, but lock stitch the lining to the main fabric first and tack round all the edges to hold the pieces together.

BINDING AN INTERLINED CURTAIN

1. Cut and join enough strips of fabric 11 cm (4¼ in) wide, to bind all edges.

2. Place the curtain fabric on to the worktable and trim away the selvedge. If your curtains are small and you are using lightweight interlining, lock stitch the interlining to the curtain fabric and treat as one piece. Pin the binding to the curtain edge from the heading towards the hem. Stop pinning 9.5 cm (3½ in) from the hem. Fold the edging over at a right angle and continue pinning parallel with the hem.

3. Stitch along the leading edge exactly 1.4 cm (just under ⅝ in) from the raw edge. It is important that the stitching line is very accurate to give an even edging. Stop at the corner 9.5 cm (3½ in) from the hem edge and secure the stitching. Fold the flap over and continue to stitch along the other side, starting 1.5 cm (⅝ in) from the leading edge. The stitches should meet at the corner.

4. Working from the front, press the binding away from the curtain. Fold the binding to the back of the curtain, measuring from the front 1.5 cm (⅝ in) all along as you pin. Carefully mitre the corner at the front.

5. Fold over and mitre the back corner. Trim the binding on the leading edge only to 6 cm (2¼ in), leaving the hem.

Continue to make up the curtain following instructions on pages 156–57. Stitch the lining to leave 1.5 cm (⅝ in) of edging visible.

6. Herringbone stitch the hem and long stitch the sides to the interlining. Continue to make curtains following the instructions on pages 156–57, stitching the lining and leaving just 1.5 cm (⅝ in) visible.

BASIC INFORMATION

Measuring and estimating the amount of fabric you will need for any kind of soft furnishing is a vital first step and one that it is essential to take time over – whether you are making something as small as this lampshade or as large as an armchair. Always remember: planning ahead is one of the secrets of success. Combine that with careful making up and you will find that even a daunting project becomes manageable.

BEDROOMS

MEASURING AND ESTIMATING

Although there are 'standard' bed sizes these do vary slightly from manufacturer to manufacturer and often greatly from country to country. When buying fabric or bedding always take your own measurements to compare rather than relying absolutely on the usual single, double, queen and king descriptions. If you need to purchase a new bed, or have ordered one, use the manufacturer's measurement for estimating purposes but wait until you have the bed to measure exactly – even one centimetre or half an inch can make a lot of difference to the drape of a bed valance. Mattress depths too can vary by as much as 15 cm (6 in).

Always measure the bed without bedding and, where necessary, with summer and winter weight bedding to show you the allowances needed for the finished articles.

Bed sizes

	width	length
single	100 cm	190 cm
	(3 ft 3 in)	(6 ft 3 in)
double	135 cm	190 cm
	(4 ft 6 in)	(6 ft 3 in)
queen	150 cm	200 cm
	(5 ft)	(6 ft 6 in)
king	180 cm	200 cm
	(6 ft)	(6 ft 6 in)
twin,	200 cm	200 cm
zipped	(6 ft 6 in)	(6 ft 6 in)

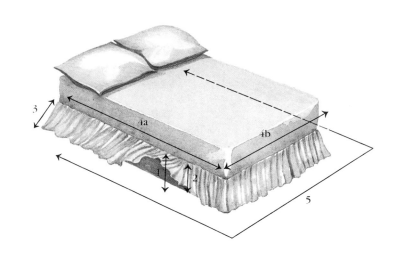

BED VALANCES

The primary function of a bed valance is to cover the part of the bed underneath the mattress. Some bed frames are works of art in their own right and need not be covered, but often unattractive material covering the divan base and any ugly metal or wooden bed frames can be covered with a skirt.

First, a 'platform' of lining, calico or other inexpensive but sturdy fabric is made to fit exactly over the bed base, under the mattress and then the 'skirt' which may be straight, pleated or gathered is stitched to the platform.

The length of the skirt will be determined primarily by the height of the bed base, but can be made overlong to drape on to the floor. If you are using the space under the bed for storage, either open or with divan drawers, you will need to be able to lift the valance for easy access. In this case, a gathered skirt will be practical but if you prefer a tailored style, then make false pleats with flaps of fabric which can be lifted easily.

To fit a valance to a bed with posts or footboards you will need to make three separate skirts, one for each side and one for the end, leaving space at the corner for the platform to fit around the leg.

Measure (see above)
1. Top of bed base to the floor.
2. Top of bed base to the bottom of the bed base.
3. Valance skirt drape from top of bed base to the floor.
4. Valance platform length (4a) and width (4b).
5. Measure around the end of the bed and the two sides.

Estimate
Platform: Allow to join your fabric widths. Seam as necessary to keep a centre width of fabric with joins at either side.
Border: Allow three cuts of the main fabric 15 cm (6 in) plus 2 cm (⅝ in) seam allowances for two lengths and one width.
Skirt: Allow fullness for pleating the whole skirt or corners only, or for gathering. Divide the total by the width of your fabric to find the number of cuts needed. Add 6 cm (2¼ in) to the skirt length for seam allowances.

PILLOWS

These vary from country to country, but tend to be standard within each country. 'Continental'-style pillows are large and square and usually measure between 65 and 75 cm (26 and 30 in). Choose light fillings which will fluff up easily but still retain good body. Make covers with approximately 1 cm (½ in) allowance all round. Pillow shams should be made with a little more allowance, as they will be removed daily and need to be as convenient as possible to handle.

Choose the length of your bed valance and curtains to be in keeping with the general style of the room and furnishings. Here, the short valance allows the antique bed frame to dominate and confirms the country style, with corded grass flooring and antique rugs. Tablecloths should either be very short to show the legs, or fall to puddle on to the floor.

TABLES AND DRESSING TABLES

Where space is limited, cloths should finish just touching the floor to prevent the cloth being caught, but if there is room, just drape the fabric on to the floor for a more extravagant effect.

Measure
1. Table top to floor.
2. Table top to floor but allowing for a) normal drape or
b) overlong drape.
3. Table diameter.

Estimate
For a normal drape, you must add measurement 1 + 3 + 2a; for an overlong cloth, add 1 + 3 + 2b.

Always estimate enough fabric to allow the centre panel to be a complete width with part widths to either side. Measure the table diameter (3), add seam allowances and divide by the width of your fabric to find the number of cuts required.

For a fitted top or dressing table, you will need to make an accurate template using newspaper or brown paper. The skirt will either fit from the front of the table with touch and close tape, or from under the table top with curtain track. In either case, take two measurements, one for the hook drop or top of tape and one for the overall drop. Allow at least double fullness of fabric for the skirt.

Two skirts are more practical than a single one, as they allow easier access to the storage space underneath.

BEDCOVERS

Bedcovers fall into two general categories – fitted and throwover, both of which may be made to fall to the floor or to stop short to show the bed legs.

All bedcovers need to be measured over your normal bedlinen, which will alter depending upon the time of year. Throwover covers may be plainly finished with a straight binding or border, or with more detail such as fringes which need to be considered when measurements are taken. All four corners may be square or the ends can be rounded. Fitted covers are made in two pieces, a top to fit the top of the bed and a skirt stitched around the three free sides.

Pillow allowances

Pillows need to be either tucked in tidily or covered with decorative covers and displayed on top of the bedcover.

There are three ways to make allowances for pillows which lay under the cover.

● Make a separate flap of fabric stitched to the top of the bedcover, long enough to fold up, over the pillows and then to tuck underneath.

● Extend the width and length to allow the bedcover to be tucked in under the pillows and to drop down over the sides (Fig i).

● To include a gusset, measure the height and length of your pillows and cut a template to fit. Add seam allowances and stitch to the bedcover top as shown (Fig ii).

Measure

For throwover:

1. Bedcover length (short to cover the top of the valance or bed frame, or long to reach to the floor).

2. Bedcover width (short or long).

For fitted:

3. The top of the bed, both length and width.

4. Around the sides and end of the bed for the skirt total.

Estimate

If a throwover, measure the width and length as described above. If fitted, measure the top only. Divide the total width by the width of your fabric to find the number of cuts needed. Always allow the centre panel to be a full width of fabric with seams to either side.

Make allowance for pillow flaps or tuck-ins as required (see pillow allowances, above). For a fitted cover, allow fullness for gathers or pleats and divide by the fabric width to find the number of cuts needed. Seam allowances of 2 cm (¾ in) for the top and 4 cm (1½ in) for the hem should be added.

Standard duvet sizes

	width	length
single	140 cm (56 in)	200 cm (78 in)
double	200 cm (78 in)	200 cm (78 in)
queen	210 cm (86 in)	220 cm (90 in)
king	240 cm (96 in)	220 cm (90 in)
superking	260 cm (104 in)	220 cm (90 in)

Fig i

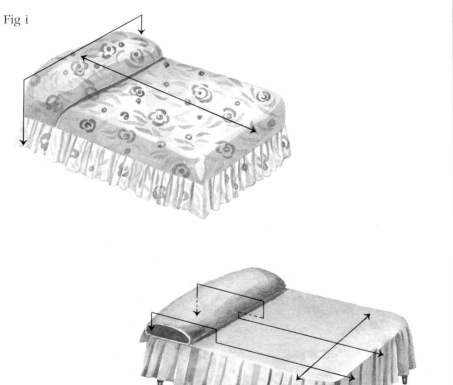

Fig ii

FOUR POSTERS
AND HALF TESTERS

You will usually need one curtain to fit behind the bed head and either four bed curtains for a four poster arrangement or two side curtains for a half tester.

If you are refurbishing an existing frame you will probably be able to follow the original fittings to find the sizes. Also decide whether you want to be able to close the curtains around a four poster bed. The amount of fullness you should allow will depend on the period of the bed. A substantial bed should have curtains which are heavy but not over full. A light, metal frame can take up to four times fullness of fine fabrics.

A simple four poster bed arrangement can be made by fitting a wooden frame to the ceiling, allowing enough depth on the wood to include fittings for curtains, ceiling drape and outer pelmet. Sometimes a bed is of a suitable design to allow poles or square sections to be fitted to each corner. Discuss your ideas with a local carpenter who will advise the best fixing methods for your room and, if possible, show examples which attract you.

Allow the frame to be roughly 15 cm (6 in) larger all round than the bed to allow adequate space for bedding and curtains.

A half tester or canopy arrangement can be put together relatively easily. You will need to design a 'pelmet board' shape cut from 15 mm (⅝ in) board, approximately 15 cm (6 in) wider

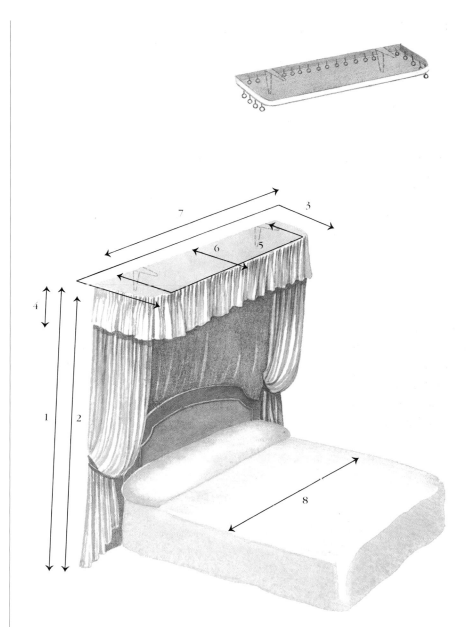

than the bed and up to 70 cm (27 in) deep. This will be fitted into the ceiling or lower, on brackets with chains to the ceiling, keeping the front level. The board should be covered with fabric. Screw eyes can be fitted at 5 cm (2 in) intervals around the back and sides to take the curtains and a fabric pelmet fitted with touch and close tape around the front will cover the unsightly fittings.

Measure (see above)

Half tester curtains:

1. The overall drop.

2. Hook drop.

3. The finished width of the back and side curtains.

Pelmets:

4. Overall drop of pelmet.

5. Pelmet finished width.

6. Canopy depth.

7. Canopy width.

8. Bed width.

Estimate

Curtains: Allow double to four times fullness for each curtain, as appropriate for your bed. The 'lining' or inner curtains are as important as the outer, so fabric needs to be chosen and estimated with equal care. The curtain behind the bed head may be lined for extra body with a neutral curtain lining.

Pelmets: If you have an inner and an outer pelmet, make sure that they both balance at the hemline. Estimate fabric as for mini-curtains, bound or finished to match the side curtains.

CORONAS

Metal or wooden corona frames should be fitted to the back wall or centrally over the bed before measurements are taken. You will need to choose whether to leave the centre open or to make a wooden board to fit inside from which to hang the canopy curtains. Or, if you need to make your own corona, then make a wooden canopy top in the same manner as a tester board which will need a pelmet to cover the front and sides. Corona curtains need to hang so that they sit on the floor across the back of the bed, but they may drape back in waterfall manner at the sides.

Both back and side curtains should be lined, but need not be interlined. If the whole is interlined it can be extremely heavy to work with, so a good compromise is to interline the side curtains only and to line the back curtain with curtain lining.

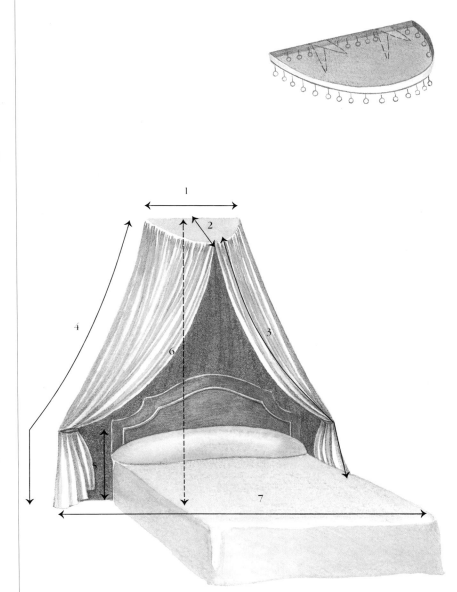

Measure (see above)

1. Corona width
2. Corona depth.
3. The front edge of the curtain to the top of the waterfall drape.
4. The side curtain from the top of the corona over the holdback fitting to the floor.
5. The back of the side curtain to the floor.
6. Back curtain, from the top to the floor.
7. Holdback to holdback.

Estimate

Curtains: Single bed – allow two widths of fabric for the back lining, four widths for the inner curtain and one width for each outer curtain. Double – three widths for the back lining, one-and-a-half widths for each outer curtain, six widths for the inner fabric. King size – five widths for the back lining, one-and-a-half widths for each outer curtain, eight widths for the inner fabric.

BLINDS

MEASURING

Once you have chosen the design of the blind and the position of the fittings, take accurate measurements to find the finished width and the overall drop. Final measurements can only be taken once the fittings are in place, but an estimate will enable you to order the fabric required.

If the building is newly built and access to the window is not possible, use the builder's drawings to estimate fabrics, but leave the making up until all building works are complete.

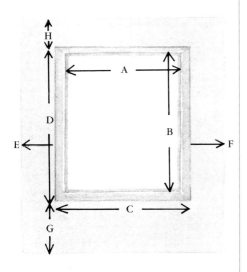

A = width of window frame, B = height of window frame, C = width of window reveal, D = height of window reveal, E = space to the left, F = space to the right, G = space below the sill, H = space above the reveal

As all blinds need to be raised and lowered without interruption, they need to be made exactly 'square'. Very few windows have four corners which are absolute right angles, so use a set square or spirit level to determine the top

line. Lightly pencil the top line on the frame or wall from which the measurements will be taken and to which the batten will be fitted. Measure at 20 cm (8 in) intervals both the width and the drop. The narrowest or shortest measurement is the one which you must use to be sure that the blind can be raised and lowered without trouble.

Special care needs to be taken with cottage or very old windows, where the opening or blind space may vary considerably with uneven walls and plastering.

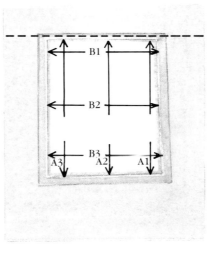

A1 = 102 cm (40 in), B1 = 64 cm (25 in),
A2 = 102.5 cm (40¼ in), B2 = 65 cm (25½ in),
A3 = 103 cm (40½ in), B3 = 64 cm (25 in).
So the blind should be made 102 × 64 cm (40 × 25 in)

Most blinds can be made to fit windows with shaped tops, for example, arches, although round windows are more difficult.

The easiest arched tops to work with have a fairly shallow curve. The blind will only pull up to the bottom of the curve, so consider the amount of available light which might be taken away.

You will need to mark a

horizontal line as near to the bottom of the arched shape as possible. Cut a paper template of

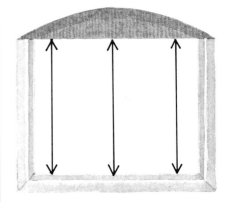

this arch, using the line you've just drawn as the bottom of the template. Measure from this line to the sill, or bottom of the blind.

If you want to make cascade, Austrian or festoon blinds, you will need to know how full they will be. Again use a strip of fabric, piece of string or length of lightweight chain and tape this to the window to see the sort of hem shape you can make (below). When you are happy with the shape, remove the tape and measure the total length and the length of each swag. This will be the finished width, which is the width the blind needs to be made.

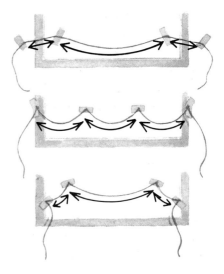

ESTIMATING FOR FABRIC

Regardless of the size of your window, each style of blind will require a different quantity of fabric depending on the style of blind you choose. A rolled-up blind, for example, will need much less fabric than a festoon blind – which can use up to 200 per cent more width and 300 per cent more depth than the window measurement. The cost of the fabric may determine your choice of blind, although the style of room and furnishings will be your first guide.

Use the following examples to help you estimate the amount of fabric you will require for each blind treatment.

ROMAN BLINDS

Decide whether the blind is to fit inside the window reveal, against the frame or outside the reveal, to the wall or an outer frame. To the finished width and the overall drop add 12 cm (4¾ in) for the side turnings and 6 cm (2¼ in) for the hem, plus heading allowance of 2–3 cm (¾–1¼ in).

1. To determine amount of fabric:
Example – finished width 150 cm (60 in) and overall drop 200 cm (79 in):

Each cut length will be:
200 cm + 3 cm + 6 cm = 209 cm (79 in + 1¼ in + 2 ¼ in = 82½ in)
The number of widths needed will depend on the width of your fabric, say 130 cm (51 in).
So, 150 cm + 12 cm = 162 cm ÷ 130 cm = 1.24 (60 in + 4¾ in = 64¾ ÷ 51 in = 1.25), say 2.
2 × 209 cm = 418 cm (2 × 82½ in = 165 in or 4½ yd).

2. You will now need to determine the size of the folds:
This will affect the amount of space taken up by the blind when it is pulled up. As a general rule of thumb, aim to make a blind which will take up approximately 17–19 cm (7–7½ in) of space when folded up.

Bear in mind that you will be stitching a rod at the top of each fold. The distance between the rods will be 30–34 cm (12–13½ in). The lowest section should be 1–2 cm (⅜–¾ in) more than half the distance between each rod.

Take the finished drop of the blind and deduct 2 cm (¾ in). Divide the rest by approximately 15 cm (6 in). You will need an uneven number, so try dividing by amounts between 15–17 cm (6–7 in) until you have a satisfactory figure.
Example: Finished length of blind will be 116 cm (45½ in)
116 cm – 2cm = 114 cm (45½ in – ¾ in = 44¾ in)
114 cm ÷ 15 cm = 7.60 cm (44¾ in ÷] 6 in = 7½ in)
Using 7 as the nearest uneven number, 114 cm ÷ 7 cm = 16.29 cm (44¾ in ÷ 7 in = 6½ in.
The folds of the blind will be 16.29 cm + 2 cm (6½ in + ¾ in) for the lower section and 32.58 cm (12½ in) for each of the other sections. Round these figures up to 18.3 cm and 32.6 cm (7 in and 13 in).

This example requires three folds and therefore three rods. (The lining cuts will need to include 6 cm (2¼ in) extra for each rod pocket.)

CASCADE BLINDS

To the finished width and overall drop measurements you will need to add 20–24 cm (8–9½ in) for the side turnings and 12–17 cm (4¾–6¾ in) for the hem, plus heading allowances. Add a further 3 cm per 50 cm (1¼ in per 20 in) on average, or 5 cm (2 in) for each scallop to give a little fullness.

1. To calculate fullness needed:
Example: the blind finished width is 140 cm (55 in) with three scallops of 34 cm (14 in) and two sides of 19 cm (7½ in).
Add the side turning allowances to the width:
140 cm + 22 cm + 22 cm = 184 cm (55 in + 9 in + 9 in = 73 in)
Add fullness (5 cm/2 in either side of each scallop):
4 × 5 = 20 cm + 184 cm = 204 cm
Divide this figure by the width of the fabric, say 135 cm (53 in).
204 cm ÷ 135 cm = 1.5 (80 in ÷ 53 in = 1.5)
so allow two widths of fabric for each blind.
The overall drop required is 185 cm (73 in)
Add the hem and heading allowances
185 cm + 12 cm + 6 cm = 203 cm (73 in + 4¾ in + 2¼ in = 80 in)
So you will need two lengths of 203 cm (80 in) 2 × 203 cm = 406 cm (2 × 80 in = 160 in.
Allow 4.5 m (4½ yd) of fabric

FESTOON BLINDS

Festoon blinds have most of their fullness in the length, some have a little fullness in the width and some are also gathered widthwise. You must choose the number of swags, the finished width of the blind and the fullness for each swag. Add 6 cm (2¼ in) for each side turning. Add the heading allowance and 2 cm (¾ in) to the length.

Example: finished width 128 cm (50 in) and overall drop of 170 cm (67 in). The festoon blind will have four swags with one and a half times fullness across the width and double the fullness in the length.
Each cut length will be:
170 cm × 2 cm = 340 cm + 6 cm headings + 2 cm hem = 348 cm
(67 in × 2 = 134 in + 2¼ in + ¾ in = 137 in)

For the swags:

32 cm × 1.5 = 48 cm × 4 = 192 cm + sides 12 cm + turnings 12 cm = 226 cm (12½ in × 1.5 = 18¾ in × 4 = 75 in + 4¾ in + 4¾ in = 84½ in)
Divide by the width of your fabric, say 130 cm (51 in):
226 ÷ 130 = 1.73 (84½ in ÷ 51 in = 1.65 in)
So you will need two lengths of 348 cm (137 in) = 696 cm (274 in)
Allow 7 m (7½ yd) of fabric.

LONDON BLINDS

From your plan you will know how many swags to allow. Pleats should require approximately the same again.
Example: overall drop 200 cm (79 in), finished width 130 cm (51 in) with three swags of 32 cm (12½ in) and two sides of 18 cm (7 in).
Each cut length will be:
200 cm + hems 10 cm + headings 2–3 cm = 213 cm
(79 in + 4 in + ¾ – 1¼ in = 84 in)
Swags: 3 × 32 cm = 96 cm + sides 36 cm + turnings 36 cm + pleats [4 × 30 cm = 120 cm] = 288 cm
(3 × 12½ in = 37½ in + 14 in + 14 in + pleats [4 × 12 in = 48 in] = 113½ in
Divide by the fabric width, say 130 cm (51 in):
288 cm ÷ 130 cm = 2.21 (113½ in ÷ 51 in = 2.22)
So you will need three lengths of 213 cm (84 in) = 639 cm (252 in)
Allow 6.5 m (7 yd) of fabric.

PATTERN REPEATS

Each cut length must include complete pattern repeats.
Example: Length needed 200 cm (79 in), pattern repeat 45 cm (18 in). Divide the length by the pattern repeat: 200 cm ÷ 45 cm = 4.44 (79 in ÷ 18 in = 4.38)
so 5 pattern repeats will be needed for each cut, making each length 45 cm × 5 = 225 cm (18 in × 5 = 90 in)

AUSTRIAN BLINDS

Austrian blinds are really pull-up curtains, with fullness added to the width and gathers or pleats incorporated at the heading to fit the batten width. Approximately 30 cm (12 in) added to the overall drop allows the bottom edge to remain swagged when the blind is lowered. Add approximately 12 cm (4¾ in) for the side turnings.

Example: finished width 130 cm (50 in), overall drop 200 cm (79 in):
Each cut length will be:
200 cm + 30 cm + hem 12 cm + heading 6 cm = 248 cm (79 in + 12 in + 4¾ in + 2¼ in = 98 in).
From the plan you will know how many swags and how much fullness each will have.

For this example, the blind has five swags of 30 cm (12 in), two sides of 10 cm (4 in), and the draped cord shows that each swag should have a 50 cm curve (20 in).
Swags: 50 cm × 5 = 250 cm + sides 10 cm × 2 – 20 cm + turnings of 20 cm = 290 cm (20 in × 5 = 100 in + 4 in × 2 = 8 in + 8 in = 116 in).
Divide this measurement by the width of your fabric (say, 130 cm (51 in) to determine the number of widths
290 cm ÷ 130 cm = 2.23 (116 in ÷ 51 in = 2.27
So you will need three lengths of 248 cm (98 in) = 744 cm (294 in)
Allow 7.5 m (8½ yd) of fabric.

LIVING ROOMS

MEASURING AND ESTIMATING

Careful planning and cutting out is essential if your loose covers are to be successful.

ARMCHAIR

Plan your pieces (see right) on to paper to make best use of the fabric width to estimate the amount needed. With a patterned fabric, it is best to mark the paper into sections to show the repeat and the pattern size. Cushions should be planned so that backs and fronts are the same and that each one is reversible or reversible with each other. The shape of the sofa or chair will dictate the reversibility of cushions.

DINING OR SIDE CHAIR

Measure the chair at the widest and highest points, following this list as a guide.

Inside back   – width
                – length + tuck in
Outside back – width
                – length to floor or
                top of skirt
Seat   – front width
                – back width
                – front to back +
                tuck-in
Skirt   – to floor
                – all around

Add 6 cm (2¼ in) all around for seam allowances. Allow 15 cm (6 in) for the tuck-in at the back of the seat, and 20 cm (8 in) for the

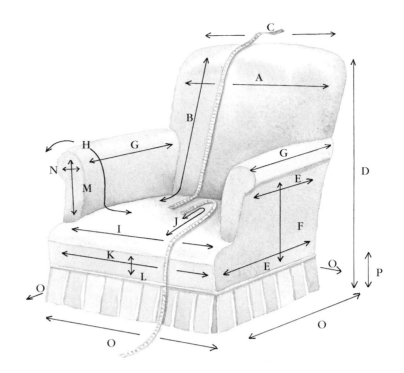

Pieces to measure

Inside back	A – width		H – length over arm +
	B – length+ tuck-in		tuck-in
Outside back	C – width	Seat	I – width + tuck-in
	D – length to valance or		J – length + tuck-in
	floor	Front gusset	K – width
Outside arm	E – width, measure top		L – depth
	and bottom	Front arm	M – height
	F – depth		N – width
Inside arm	G – width, measure top	Sides	O – around the frame
	and bottom	Valance	P – depth of valance

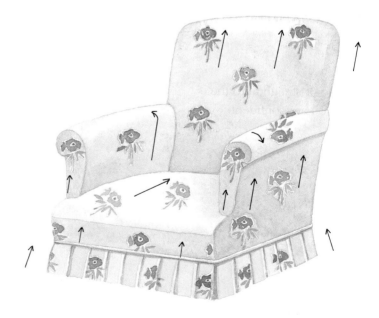

Direction of pattern

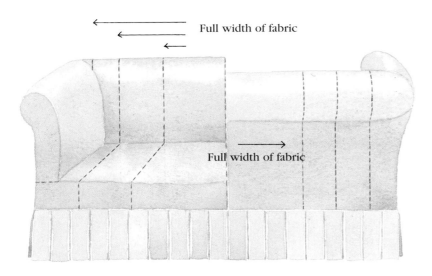

Full width of fabric

Full width of fabric

Seam positions

flap under the chair seat. Decide whether you want to have a valance around the chair seat, and if so, the style and fullness. Also consider whether to have any other decoration.

Plan these pieces on to graph paper to calculate the fabric needed. Make allowance for any pattern repeat and choose the pattern position on the chair back and seat.

CUTTING OUT

Cut out the pieces of fabric as planned. Use calico if you are making a toile or straight into the top cover if you are confident. Make up enough piping cord for the whole job.

Using the tape measure, place a vertical row of pins to mark the centre line of the inside back, outside back, front and seat.

WOODEN CHAIRS

Squab cushions add a decorative, welcoming touch to a wooden

chair seat, but the primary function is to make a hard chair seat more comfortable. Foam or rubberised hair with a wadding wrap are the best padding solutions for this type of cushion.

You will need to cut a template from the actual chair seat to use as an accurate pattern for the seat shapes. Either paper, or tightly woven cotton are suitable, but for

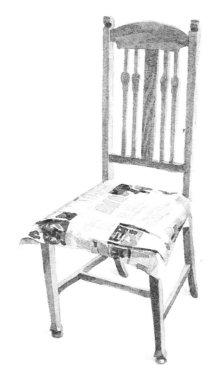

this purpose, I prefer newspaper, which is soft enough to fold and tear easily to fit around difficult leg and arm interruptions. A thick pencil is useful to mark the edges of the seat on to the paper, and sticky tape will help hold the folds and tears in place. I then transfer this pattern to heavier brown paper from which I cut the fabric and pad patterns.

Tape paper to the back, front and sides of the chair seat. Bend the paper along the shaped seat and confirm the line with a thick pencil. Tear and fold the paper around the arms and legs to give you a really accurate shape. Remember, you can always stick a bit of paper back on if you over-cut by accident. The important thing is to fit the paper surely enough to gain an accurate template from which to cut your final pattern.

ACCESSORIES

MEASURING AND ESTIMATING

TABLECLOTHS

Long cloths should be made with due consideration to the drape of the folds and whether the cloth should finish above the floor or whether it should puddle a little.

Round tablecloths

The diameter of a round cloth should be equal to the height of the table x two, plus the diameter of the table top. Hold the tape measure at the top of the table and then at an angle to estimate the length of the drape.

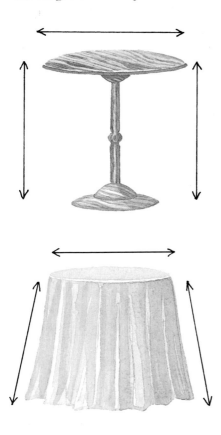

Oval tablecloths

The only way to make an accurate tablecloth for an oval table is to create a template of the top and then to add the length of the drop all around.

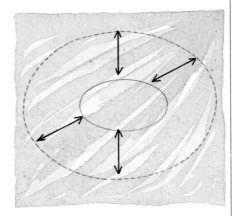

Square tablecloths

The corners of square cloths always drop below the natural bottom line of the cloth, which looks attractive if the cloth is short, but could be a hazard for a floor-length cloth. To remove the point, drape the fabric over the table and pin the folds at each corner. Draw lightly around the straight sides. Trim away the fabric and cut a straight edge in line with the marks, taking any hem allowance into consideration.

Hexagonal and octagonal tablecloths

Make a template of the table top and add the drop measurements all around. The resulting hemline will be many short, straight edges.

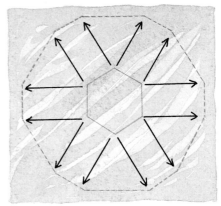

SEAMS

Always plan seams where they will be least obvious, for example, within a corner pleat, or along the edge of a square table. On round or oval tables try to make a seam which falls in with the draping where it will be less noticeable.

NAPKINS

Standard lunchtime napkins are approximately 40 cm (16 in) square, dinner napkins will need to be a minimum of 50 cm (20 in) square. Plan the cutting lines and try to fit three smaller napkins across the width of the fabric.

LAMPSHADES

Lampshade measurements are always given in the same order: top/slope/base.

The top and bottom measurements are all frame diameter measurements.

For gathered shades, allow for the heading and for the drop beneath the shade.

As a general rule, the diameter of the base of the frame should be equal to the height of the base. Of course, in tall candle lamps this is not the case. You will find that it is usual for candle lamps to come in two sizes. Small candle lamps are 15 x 10 x 5 cm (6 x 45 x 2 in) and larger ones 20 x 15 x 5 cm (8 x 6 x 2 in). Both of these fit the standard bulb clip fitting. In empire or drum shades the

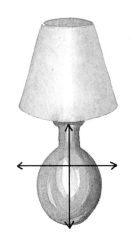

diameter of the top and bottom rings is not too far apart; there is a large difference in coolie shacks.

Preparing the frame

Most frames which are now available have been treated and finished with a plastic coating in white or off-white. If there are any lumps or bumps, sand them smooth. Check to see that there are no holes – if there are, dab on some enamel or household gloss paint and leave to dry. Frames must be completely sealed, as most cotton and silk shades can be washed gently.

Frames can always be painted with gloss paint if you want to change the colour. For instance, if you should choose to make a dark red shade without a lining, the white frame beneath will look ugly and might show through.

Binding the frame

You will need to bind the top and bottom rings with narrow tape to provide a surface into which to pin and stitch.

Cut off a length of tape approximately three times the length to be covered. Roll it up into a ball and keep in the palm of your hand.

The last thing you want is lengths of tape flapping around.

You need to keep the tape as taut as possible, because if the binding is loose, the fabric which is stitched to the binding will be able to twist around and any pleats will distort.

1. Begin by holding the top of the shade uppermost and one strut facing you, keeping the remainder of the frame resting on your lap. Starting at the top of one strut, twist the tape around it as shown.

2. Overlap each twist by approximately one third. Keep one finger on the last twist at all times, sliding your finger around the ring as you go. Finish where you started with a figure of eight loop. Pull tight and secure with a couple of back stitches. Bind the bottom ring in the same way.

CUSHIONS

For a squab cushion pad, cut a piece of foam or rubberised hair to the template and follow the instructions below.

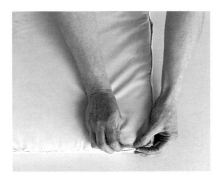

1. Wrap the pad with the wadding or interlining, leaving enough at each edge to fold up over the sides, starting and finishing at the back to keep the front seam-free. Fold the sides and back to one edge, trim away excess so that the pad is now enclosed. Stitch interlining together or cover the wadding with calico. Pull the top and bottom together at the back and stitch the raw edges together.

2. Cover this pad with lining in the same way, making a gusset at either end. Hand stitch all around three sides to enclose the pad.

SCATTER CUSHIONS

Scatter cushions need to be soft and comfortable, to be able to mould around the body easily. The very best filling is a mix of down and feather, but economy dictates that most cushions will have a large percentage of feathers. Down, being soft and fluffy, will respond to being plumped up for as many years as you wish – the tiny fibres fill with air immediately. If there is a chance of finding an eiderdown from a parent or grandparent which may be externally damaged, use the filling for your best cushions.

Basic feather fillings are curled poultry feathers which have been cured and wrapped in a feather-proof ticking case. In time, the feathers will uncurl and once flat have little means of trapping air. It is a false economy to re-stuff an old cushion – it will just become heavy and flatten even more quickly. Replace the pad. If you are allergic to feathers then a fibre filling is a reasonable alternative. Fibre will never quite give the fullness of a feather pad and may well become misshapen in a relatively short period of time.

Avoid kapok or foam chip fillings as these are always lumpy.

Many sizes and shapes of pad are readily available from large department stores and any unusual or over-sized pads may be ordered through a soft furnishings specialist or interior decorator. Choose your pads carefully. If you want to make a cushion to fit into the small of the back, test an old one to find the size which is most comfortable once it has been flattened. Always scale the cushion size to the sofa size. Some modern sofas are very deep, and normal 43 cm (17 in) cushions will look completely lost.

It is fun to use very large cushions or very small cushions for decoration. Experiment with groupings and sizes. Perhaps a pile of three or four large cushions on the floor or a small 30 cm (12 in) cushion sitting at the back of a formal side chair.

Scatter cushions are accessories and although used for comfort at times, for the most part of the day, the function is purely decorative. It doesn't much matter which cushion is used where once a room is full of people, but for first impressions each cushion should be in its place.

Before you can choose the fabrics, the colours and the pad sizes, you will need to have chosen the room style. You might prefer a formal setting, with structured, tailored cushions, or you might wish to introduce a contrast by adding frills and cords. In either case, the size for pad and finish will be very important as each cushion will be a statement, and need to be chosen with the scale of the room and furniture in mind. Use a pillow or other cushions and offcuts of fabric to help you plan.

If you have chosen an informal room, then a mix of pad sizes will be needed: large and small squares and rectangles with perhaps bolsters and round box cushions. Again, planning is the reason for success. The rule of thumb is to buy a pad size 2.5 cm (1 in) larger than the cover size.

CURTAINS

MEASURING AND PLANNING

The most successful window treatments have been carefully considered and designed before the fabric has even been purchased. Once you have taken accurate window measurements (see right) round them up or down to the nearest 5 mm (¼ in) and transfer them to graph paper. If you have neither scale rulers nor graph paper, work with a very simple scale, say, 1 cm = 10 cm or 1 in = 10 in, and a normal ruler.

Mark the room height, the position of the window and the space around the window. If there is a bay, beam or other obstacle, mark this also. Please don't be put off if you have no drawing experience. The examples here are deliberately simple to give you the confidence to try.

You will need tracing paper to place over your window plan and paper clips to hold them together. Experiment by drawing different curtains and fitting positions: long, short, with or without pelmets, formal or gathered headings, etc. You will soon begin to formulate suitable ideas.

Once you have a fairly definite concept, draw the window again, tidying up the measurements and draw the design as accurately as you can. Try to mark exactly where the fittings should be – how far to the side of the window and how far above. If you want to make a pelmet, mark the top, sides and centre and shape the edge roughly.

Translate your ideas to the window by marking the walls around with a soft pencil and stand back to look. You will need to make an accurate template for a pelmet (see page 74). Most fittings can be cut to size, so ask someone to hold them in place for you to see what they will look like before they are finally fitted.

TAKING ACCURATE MEASUREMENTS

Measure the width and height at least three times so that you are aware if the window is not 'square' and if the floor or ceiling slopes.

Measurements to take:
- From the top of the frame or reveal to the floor.
- From the ceiling (or under the cornice) to the top of the window.
- From the ceiling to the floor.
- The window width inside – noting any possible problems, eg, telephone sockets, etc.
- The window width outside.
- Measure the distance available all around the window for the curtain stack-back, avoiding pictures, bookcases, etc.

Stand back and check for any ugly fitments which might need to be covered. Measure and note unsightly double-glazing fittings, odd bits of wood, etc. Decide whether you need blinds and/or pelmets or fixed curtain headings. Plan how – and exactly where – they should be positioned. If a pelmet is to be used, make a template and tape it into position to check how it will look.

For curtains to hang outside reveal

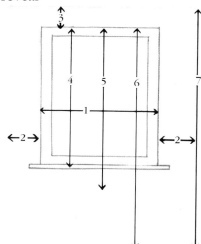

1 width of window
2 width of stack-back
3 top of architrave to ceiling
4 top of architrave to sill
5 top of architrave to below sill
6 top of architrave to floor
7 ceiling to floor

For curtains to hang inside reveal

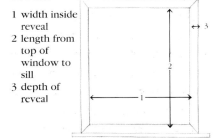

1 width inside reveal
2 length from top of window to sill
3 depth of reveal

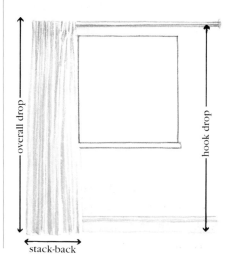

overall drop

hook drop

stack-back

ESTIMATING FOR CURTAINS

Heading Requirements

Heading Type	Fullness Required
Gathered headings	
Tape	1.75 – 2.25
Ties	1.25 – 2.50
Handsewn	2.50 – 3.00
Bunched	2.25 – 2.50
Smocked	2.50 – 3.50
Pencil pleated	2.50 – 2.75
Hand Pleated	
Triple (French)	2.25 – 2.75
Goblets	2.25 – 2.50
Folded	
Pocket	2.00 – 3.00
Voiles	2.50 – 3.00

Most curtains look best with at least double fullness, but this may be reduced for short curtains which do not need the weight to hang well. If stack-back space is restricted, pleated headings will hold the curtain back into the smallest space. Allow only 1¼ to 1½ times fullness for a heavy fabric or one with a dominant design which needs to be seen.

Heading Allowances

Bunched

Allow enough for a 10–12 cm (4–4¾ in) 'bunch' depending on the thickness of the fabric. Allow the hook drop plus 25–50 cm (10–20 in).

Frilled

Allow the frill above the hook drop and back to fit under the tape.

Allow the hook drop plus 12 cm (4½ in) for a 6 cm (2¼ in) frill, 16 cm (6½ in) for an 8 cm (3¼ in) frill, etc.

Pencil pleated

Allow the depth of the pleats.
Allow the overall drop plus 6–8 cm (2¼–3¼ in).

Pocket headings

For voiles, allow 2 cm (¾ in) for the pocket and 2 cm (¾ in) above.
Allow the overall drop plus 8 cm (3¼ in).

Bound headings

No allowance needed.
Overall drop, no extra.

Smocked

Allow the depth of the smocking pattern.
Allow the overall drop plus the depth of the smocking pattern.

Goblet/triple pleats

Allow double the depth of the pleat.
Allow the overall drop plus 20 cm (8 in) for a 10 cm (4 in) pleat.
Allow the overall drop plus 30 cm (12 in) for a 15 cm (6 in) pleat.

Hem Allowances

Unlined curtains	16 cm (6¼ in)
Lined curtains	16 cm (6¼ in)
Lined, bound hems, plain lining	8 cm (3¼ in)
Lined, bound hems, contrast lining	No extra fabric
Interlined curtains	12 cm (4¾ in)
Voile curtains	8–12 cm (3¼–4¾ in)

ESTIMATING FOR FABRIC

The quantity of fabric needed for each window is relative to the style of curtaining which you wish to make. The three factors are: the headings style, the fullness, and the curtain length. You will have already chosen your window treatment style following the guidelines on page 12 and from this you will know the fittings width and the overall drop of the curtains. The hook drop is the measurement from the top of the curtain hook and the bottom of the curtain fitting, to the hemline. The overall drop is from the top of the heading to the hemline. You will need to estimate these measurements from your plan, until the fittings are in position. The overall drop is from the top of the heading to the hemline.

Make allowances for any changes – for instance, if cupboards are to be fitted close to the window, or a possible change of flooring. Use the following as a guide.

Each Length

1. Find the overall drop

ceiling to floorboards	270 cm	(106 in)
less allowance for carpet of 2 cm (¾ in)	268 cm	(105¼ in)
less allowance for pelmet board of 2 cm (¾ in)	266 cm	(104½ in)
plus overlong hem allowance of 5 cm (2 in)	271 cm	(106½ in)

2. Add the hem and heading allowances

hem		12 cm (4¾ in)
heading		20 cm (8 in)
each cut length		303 cm (119 in)

3. Adjust for pattern repeat, if necessary

If the pattern repeat is 65 cm (25½ in)

303 cm ÷ 65 cm = 4.66
(119 in ÷ 25½ in = 4.66)
round up to 5.

Allow 5 repeats for each cut as each cut length must include complete pattern repeats.

5 × 65 cm = 325 cm
(5 × 25½ in = 127½ in)
Each cut length will need to be 325 cm (127½ in).

Note the fabric 'wastage': 325 cm (127½ in) is needed for each cut, yet only 303 cm (119 in) is actually needed for the curtain, so five pieces of 22 cm (8½ in) will be left.

At this point you can decide how best to use this spare fabric. You might decide to alter the headings, for example to have a frilled and bound heading rather than bound only, or to increase the heading fullness from frilled to bunched. Or this spare could be allocated for tiebacks, pelmets, etc, depending on the amount available.

Fabric pelmets can be very expensive, but can often be cut from the same piece of fabric, with each curtain cut. Another advantage is that the pattern is already matched.

Planning the fabric in this way means that you will never have wasted pieces, and will be aware when cutting of the importance of using the fabric wisely.

If the fabric you have chosen is expensive and the estimated cuts are just over a whole repeat (i.e. 4.1 repeats) you might decide to shorten the hem or heading allowance a little. Just enough to save costs without damaging the hanging quality.

Always allow an extra pattern repeat to the total amount of fabric estimated, to allow you to start your hemline in the position on the pattern which you choose.

How Many Widths

1. Select your fitting and divide the length in half for two curtains

180 cm ÷ 2 = 90 cm
(70 in ÷ 2 = 35 in)

2. Add the side return (10 cm/4 in) and the centre overlap (10 cm/4 in)

90 cm + 10 cm + 10 cm = 110 cm
(35 in + 4 in + 4 in = 43 in)

3. Multiply by the fullness needed for your heading

110 cm × 2.5 = 275 cm
(43 in × 2.5 = 107½ in, say 108 in)

4. Divide by the width of your fabric

275 cm ÷ 135 cm = 2.04
(108 in ÷ 54 in = 2)
Therefore, use two cuts per curtain

5. Multiply the number of widths by the cut lengths

Plain fabric
303 cm × 4 = 12.12 metres
(119 in × 4 = 13¼ yd)
You will need 12.12 m (13¼ yd)

Patterned fabric
325 cm × 4 = 13 metres
+ 65 cm for extra repeat = 13.65 metres
(127½ in × 4 = 14 yd
+ 25½ in = 14¾ yd)
You will need 13.65 m (14¾ yd)

MAKING TEMPLATES

Make accurate templates of anything which might prevent drapes hanging well. Cornices will usually be above the curtaining, but sometimes the side of the pelmet will need to return on to the cornice, there might be a plate rack or picture rail or pipes obstructing the fall of the curtains.

Use brown paper and a pencil to draw around the obstruction, if possible. If not, tear the paper roughly and cut in around it accurately with a sharp knife.

Curtain Fittings

CURTAIN TRACKS

For most uses, metal tracks with plastic runners and an enclosed pull-cording system are the best.

These tracks are available in several different qualities to suit the weight and length of your curtains and are easily adaptable to 'top fit' on to a pelmet board or into the recess, or to 'face fit' to the wall, to a batten or directly on to the window frame. They are also available in telescopic lengths to suit a wide range of window sizes.

Side fittings, which hold the track to the wall, are available in several different sizes so that the track can be fitted either very close to the wall or some distance out. This facility allows the curtains to hang straight over a radiator or deep sill.

CURTAIN POLES

There are so many different types of pole and finial style available in the shops that you will be spoilt for choice.

Choose poles which can be fitted as closely to the wall as possible with brackets which have fixings above and below the pole, otherwise heavy curtains could pull the fitting away from the wall. The end brackets should be positioned so that there is approximately 3 cm (1¼ in) from the fitting to the end of the pole, just enough space for one curtain ring. The curtain will then pull right to the end of the pole.

INDEX

ACKNOWLEDGEMENTS

Thanks to all those without whom this book would not have been possible. To John for his skill with juggling light and f-stops.
For the dedication of the team at New Holland, the designers and last, but not least, my soft furnishings team.
Special thanks and appreciation to Gilda and Paul Chadd, Sarah Taylor, Blair and Mary Stewart-Wilson, Andrew and Annie Stewart,
George Stewart, Jano and Johnie Clarke, Carol Hicks, Dibby Nethercott, Heather and Nicholas Phelps Brown and Elizabeth Peck
for allowing us to photograph and so share their beautiful homes.

We would like to thank the following suppliers for their help:
Artisan for the fittings on pages 126, 130, 166, 169, 170
Bennison for pages 18, 21, 36
Calluna for the fabrics on page 80
The Cartonnage Company for accessories on pages 75, 121, 143
Chelsea Textiles for the fabrics on page 76
Designers Guild for the photograph on the back cover (left)
Pierre Frey for the fabrics on page 151 and the photographs on
pages 31 (bottom left), 167
Le Lievre for page 54 (top right)
Merchants for the fittings on page 166
Les Olivades for the fabrics on page 73
Osborne and Little for the fabrics on pages 24, 65 (bottom), 148, 162, 164
Percheron for the toile de Jouy on page 86
Weymss Houles for fittings on page 151
The White House for the pillows and bedcovers on pages 69, 75

For soft furnishings course details, contact Calluna Workshops, Hill House, Creech St Michael,
Taunton, Somerset TA3 5DP. Fax: 01823 442711